# Tire Imprint
# Evidence

ELSEVIER SERIES IN
**PRACTICAL ASPECTS OF CRIMINAL
AND FORENSIC INVESTIGATIONS**

VERNON J. GEBERTH, BBA, MPS, FBINA *Series Editor*

**Practical Homicide Investigation: Tactics, Procedures, and
Forensic Techniques**
Vernon J. Geberth

**Friction Ridge Skin: Comparison and Identification of
Fingerprints**
James F. Cowger

**Gunshot Wounds: Practical Aspects of Firearms, Ballistics, and
Forensic Techniques**
Vincent J. M. Di Maio

**Practical Fire and Arson Investigation**
John J. O'Connor

**The Sexual Exploitation of Children: A Practical Guide to Assessment,
Investigation, and Intervention**
Seth L. Goldstein

**Practical Drug Enforcement: Procedures and Administration**
Michael D. Lyman

**Interpretation of Bloodstain Evidence at Crime Scenes**
William G. Eckert and Stewart H. James

**Tire Imprint Evidence**
Peter McDonald

# Tire Imprint Evidence

**PETER McDONALD**
Formerly, Manager of Tire Design
Firestone Tire & Rubber Company
Akron, Ohio

**Elsevier**
New York • Amsterdam • London

No responsibility is assumed by the publisher for any injury and/or damage to persons or property as a matter of products liability, negligence, or otherwise, or from any use or operation of any methods, products, instructions, or ideas contained in the material herein.

Elsevier Science Publishing Co., Inc.
655 Avenue of the Americas, New York, NY 10010

Sole distributors outside the United States and Canada:

Elsevier Science Publishers B.V.
P.O. Box 211, 1000 AE Amsterdam, The Netherlands

This book is printed on acid-free paper.

Library of Congress Cataloging-in-Publication Data

McDonald, Peter.
  Tire imprint evidence / Peter McDonald.
    p. cm.—(Elsevier series in practical aspects of criminal and forensic investigations)
  Includes index.
  Bibliography: p.
  1. Motor vehicles—Tires—Identification.    I. Series.
HV8077.5.T57M33     1989
363.2'562—dc20                                             89-7733
                                                           CIP

ISBN 0-444-01456-X

Current printing (last digit):

10  9  8  7  6  5  4  3  2  1

Manufactured in the United States of America

*To my wife and family,*
*I wish to extend a very special*
*acknowledgment of their support.*

# Contents

# Preface

*Marked on the sodden soil, was the trace of a bicycle.*
*"Hurrah!" I cried. "We have it."*
*But Holmes was shaking his head, and his face was puzzled and expectant rather than joyous.*
*"A bicycle certainly, but not the bicycle," said he. "I am familiar with forty-two different impressions left by tyres. This, as you perceive, is a Dunlop, with a patch upon the outer cover. Heidegger's tyres were Palmer's, leaving longitudinal stripes. Aveling, the mathematical master, was sure upon the point. Therefore it is not Heidegger's track."*
*"The boy's, then?"*
*"Possibly, if we could prove a bicycle to have been in his possession. But this we have utterly failed to do. This track, as you perceive, was made by a rider who was going from the direction of the school."*
*"Or towards it?"*
*"No, no, my dear Watson. The more deeply sunk impression is, of course, the hind wheel, upon which the weight rests. You perceive several places where it has passed across and obliterated the more shallow mark of the front one. It was undoubtedly heading away from the school. It may or may not be connected with our inquiry, but we will follow it backwards before we go any farther."*

Arthur Conan Doyle, "The Adventure of the Priory School," 1901

Sherlock Holmes, at the beginning of the century, recognized the importance of identifying tire tread designs and observing unique accidental characteristics. He also determined the tire position and direction of travel. Today's investigators may not be so fortunate as to observe "a patch upon the outer cover." But we do have pitch sequence variations and much more to make our job easier.

The individuality of people and their fingerprints has become a well recognized forensic tool since it was introduced in 1901. Shoe prints and footprints have also become valuable evidence for the investigator. Currently, the identification of tire imprints, or "footprints," at the scene of a crime has become increasingly important in establishing that a suspect's vehicle was at a crime scene.

Most shoe prints are a pair. All the people I know wear shoes of the same design and size on each foot. They also buy them at the same time. However, many vehicle owners will replace worn or damaged tires as needed, and this can result in a vast difference in comparative worn imprints and often different designs and sizes at different wheel positions. Simply identifying more than one brand or size tire on a single vehicle can significantly affect the probability factor of that combination of tires appearing on another vehicle.

Since a vehicle is generally used when leaving the scene of a crime, a tire "footprint," or contact patch, is significant. Interestingly, a single tire "footprint" is approximately the same surface area as a large man's shoe print. However, tires generally have more than five times the load per square inch as compared to a shoe print. The resulting tire print, therefore, is often more clearly visible than a shoe print on a soft surface.

The growing awareness of valuable tire print evidence, in this mobile age, will hopefully assist investigators in their work. Unfortunately we tend to think of tires as lacking individuality—just piles of nondescript tires. It is interesting to note the similarities of shoe prints, barefoot prints, and tire footprints. The creative Wellco Military Footwear designers seemed to recognize the features of each. They have designed a boot with a velcro secured bottom that will accommodate an interchangeable tire tread sole, or a traction device sole, much like studded tires. The special "HO-CHI-MINH" barefoot sole was designed to confuse the enemy into thinking that only barefoot natives had passed. Like the interchangeable shoe sole, tire retreads can be similar and confusing.

When I first started writing this book, I intended to jump right into the subject of tire imprints and their analysis. However, it soon became obvious that I could not write about tires without first providing some fundamental information about their nomenclature, design, manufacturing, and functioning, and also some information about how they are sold. The first five chapters cover all of this briefly. If you do not read these chapters, you will find yourself lost in the later discussions, so I recommend you take a deep breath and plow your way through them. You will then be ready to understand the real subject of this book.

My wife, Linda, and I started this book in a wonderful, but very unconventional, way in this day of word processors. Many days were spent at our remote island, loading our canoe with books, writing material, and folding chairs—then paddling to a different island every day to write under the shade of a tree, then swim, and have lunch. A great way to develop thoughts. Of course one returns to the conveniences of computers and photographic facilities, but I recommend a natural setting for writing a book.

This book has been written primarily for crime investigators. However, the research techniques, standards, and procedures will no doubt be beneficial to police officers in general, crime scene specialists, forensic laboratory technicians, accident reconstruction specialists, judges, and lawyers. The full potential of tire imprint evidence has not been explored. If information presented in this book prompts crime-scene examiners, investigators, police, and the courts to recognize the significance of analyzing tire imprints correctly, then my goals will have been met.

# Acknowledgments

I wish to acknowledge and thank the many people who have assisted in making this book possible by providing photographic assistance, technical advice, or other assistance: Horace Auberry, E. H. Baker, M. M. Benick, William J. Bodziak, Roger J. Bolhouse, Roy E. Brown, K. L. Campbell, Mike Carrick, Hans P. Dara, John Davis, Sue F. DeGasperin, Addis Finney, John E. Fletcher, Ottis W. Garrett, Vernon J. Geberth, Jack E. Gieck, Robert Gosman, Byron G. Hahn, Gay Molchen, L. A. Nause, Stephen Ojena, Frank M. Placenti, Jim Rogers, Captain James Sagans, Al Snyder, Robert Taylor, David A. Thomas, Gary Truszkowski, Charles E. Waldron, Rob Warden, David F. Webster, and Fredric L. Zuch. I apologize to anyone whom I may have inadvertently omitted. In particular, I want to thank those people at Firestone who encouraged my involvement in forensic science.

# Tire Imprint
# Evidence

# A Brief History of the Tire  1

*Tires are the means to support, propel, and guide vehicles. The first tires at the turn of the century frequently lasted less than 1,000 miles. It was common to carry six spares. Today's modern tires often deliver more than 40,000 miles.*

(Kovac 1978)

The first five chapters of this book provide basic information about tires that will assist today's tire imprint examiners. The next chapters provide discussions of specific details that are useful in making tire imprint identification and case studies involving such identification processes.

The Sumerians are generally credited with inventing the wheel some 5,000 years ago. Since then, the wheel has been continually refined to meet the needs of the vehicle it supported. In 1846, Robert William Thompson obtained a patent in England for an "aerial wheel," a concept similar to today's pneumatic tire, but this invention remained unused until the pneumatic tire was reinvented by John Dunlop in 1888.

The first tires were bald, and poor roads made traction designs a necessity. In 1907, Harvey Firestone is said to have suggested the first traction design, using the words "Firestone Non-Skid." The words "Firestone" and "Non-Skid" alternated positive and negative, so that the manufacturer's identity and design name were legible in the impression (see Figure 1.1). This tread pattern gave improved traction. In addition, although it was not intentional, the varied tread elements were probably the first noise-treated design. The round shoulder was probably good for handling too, and the tread pattern was good

**Figure 1.1.** Alternating mirror image of tire name leaves legible impression. (*Courtesy of Firestone Tire & Rubber Co.*)

advertising. (If each manufacturer today identified its tires so obviously, investigators of tire imprints would find their jobs much easier.)

Goodyear's first tread design consisted of diamond-shaped elements. The company continued to use this basic design for many years. Even today, some tire manufacturers adapt basic tread features as a theme and continue that theme for many years in a variety of tread designs. Knowing this will help an investigator who is trying to identify a particular design.

As road conditions improved and major routes were paved, the early button-type tread designs were replaced by continuous-rib designs for high speed. In the 1930s, tread designs were primarily circumferential ribs of continuous tread rubber separated by grooves. Later, to improve traction on slippery surfaces, sipes (narrow slits in the tread surface) were introduced. The primary internal tire construction from before 1920 until the 1960s was bias ply, but now it is radial. "Bias" and "radial" refer to the angle of the cords in the tire plies.

The history of tires in the twentieth century has to do largely with a progression of different tire constructions and tread designs. Investigators will find that certain tread designs that are appropriate for only one type of construction are therefore a clue for identifying a specific tire.

## Tread Designs

Fortunately for the investigator, the design of the tread pattern affects the overall performance of a tire. Depending on the type of performance required and the construction used (bias, belted-bias, or radial), the tread pattern may be an indication of a specific type of vehicle. The typical circumferential zigzag tread pattern, which provides better mileage, traction, and reduces side-slippage, meets most driving requirements. However, a variety of lateral slots have been introduced for improved traction.

The tread is molded into a series of *grooves* and *ribs.* The ribs provide the wearing surfaces and the road contact that enable the driver to steer and stop. The grooves permit an easy, fast escape for water and give the tread edges a direct, positive grip on the surface being traveled. To increase the traction of any tire, the small slots called *sipes* are molded into the ribs of the tread design. As the tread area moves across the road surface, the sipes provide extra traction edges. On wet pavement they help wipe water away and thereby improve the traction (see Figure 1.2).

**Figure 1.2.** Radial tire cutaway showing ply construction. (*Courtesy of Firestone Tire & Rubber Co.*)

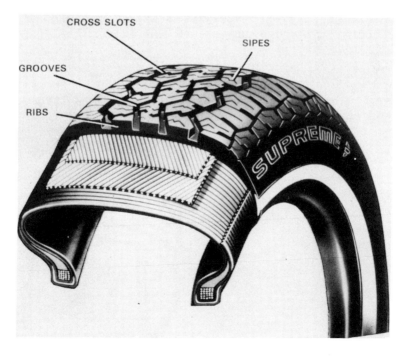

## Types of Tire Construction

There are three types of tire construction: bias construction, belted-bias construction, and radial-ply construction.

### Bias Construction

Bias (meaning on an angle) construction may be two, four, or more plies placed on top of one another in alternating directions on the bias. The tire body ply cords run from bead to bead (see Figure 1.3). This basic, simple construction provides adequate traction and mileage performance.

### Belted-Bias Construction

In belted-bias construction, the cord body is constructed as in bias construction, with the cords in the body plies running at an angle from bead to bead. However, two or more belts are then applied on top of the body plies directly under the tread area only (see Figure 1.4). Regardless of the type of cord material used, adding these high-strength, low-elongation belts lessens the stresses on the cord body greatly and stabilizes the tread area of the tire. Belted-bias construction provides better mileage and traction and greater impact and puncture resistance, compared with the conventional bias construction.

**Figure 1.3.** Bias construction. (*Courtesy of Firestone Tire & Rubber Co.*)

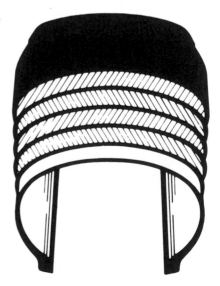

**Figure 1.4.** Belted-bias construction. (*Courtesy of Firestone Tire & Rubber Co.*)

## Radial-Ply Construction

Radial construction utilizes one or more body plies, with the cords running *in a straight line* from bead to bead. On top of these body plies are two or more belt plies, referred to as "stabilizer belts" (see Figure 1.5). These stabilizer belts prevent "squirm" in the tread area and give the tire lateral stability.

Compared with conventional bias and belted bias construction, radial-ply construction provides the most mileage, the quickest steering response, the greatest impact resistance, the best traction, the best

**Figure 1.5.** Radial-ply construction. (*Courtesy of Firestone Tire & Rubber Co.*)

cornering control, savings in fuel costs due to lower rolling resistance, and the smoothest ride at highway speeds (Firestone 1982).

Messrs. Gray and Sloper are generally credited with constructing the original radial tire in 1913, but radial-ply construction did not gain popular use in North America until the mid-1960s. Radials now account for well over 70 percent of the U.S. tire market. This figure has been steadily increasing since the early 1970s, when radials were first used as original equipment on some new cars. Consumers seem to recognize the superior performance and greater mileage of radials vs. bias or bias-belted tires.

Bias-ply-construction tires have continuous ribs for good reasons. The previous button-type traction designs would have failed at the higher speeds of today. In addition, they were noisy and rough-riding. Radial construction prevents "squirm" of the tire tread and makes practical the more open and aggressive tread designs that are common on radial tires, for today's higher speeds.

## Tire Construction and the Three Cycles

Every passenger tire, regardless of type of construction, goes through three cycles (Figure 1.6) during one complete revolution of the wheel: the contraction (or footprint) cycle, the expansion cycle, and the normal stress cycle.

Figure 1.7 shows the tread of a conventional bias-construction tire as it goes through the three stress cycles in one revolution of a wheel. The top illustration in the figure shows a normal tread. The center illustration shows how the contraction cycle squeezes the tread together as the cord pulls at opposing angles. The bottom illustration shows how the tread design expands as the cord body reverses the direction of its pull in the expansion cycle.

In a belted-bias-construction tire, the added belts under the tread greatly reduce the pull of the cord body during the contraction and expansion cycles (see Figure 1.8). The result is less scrubbing on the

**Figure 1.6.** Tires rotate through three cycles (A) contraction; (B) expansion; and (C) stress.

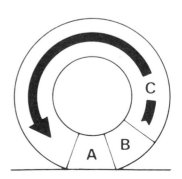

**Figure 1.7.** Bias-construction tire tread going through the three stress cycles (extreme). (*Courtesy of Firestone Tire & Rubber Co.*)

**Figure 1.8.** Belted-bias-construction tire tread going through the three stress cycles (reduced). (*Courtesy of Firestone Tire & Rubber Co.*)

**Figure 1.9.** Radial-ply construction tire tread going through the three stress cycles (minimized). (*Courtesy of Firestone Tire & Rubber Co.*)

**Figure 1.10.**   Tire designs have gone full circle.

pavement, and this is the reason belted-bias tires give better mileage than bias tires.

> In radial tires the tread area retains almost the same shape in all three cycles [Figure 1.9]. This is because radial body plies do not set up diagonal stress in the expansion and contraction cycles as do bias cord bodies. The belt plies stabilize the tread and hold it flat on the road surface. The absence of scrubbing action makes the radial tires the ultimate for long mileage (Firestone 1982).

The flexible sidewalls and rigid belts of the radial tire greatly improve tread stability. Less tread squirm has made it possible for engineers to develop more open and aggressive tread designs that can take today's high speeds. In a way, the industry has gone full circle, returning to the early button-type tread designs (Figure 1.10).

To dramatize the movement to which tire tread elements are subjected, it has been noted that each point on the average passenger tire flexes nearly 800 times per minute at 55 mph.

# Mechanics of the Tire Tread 2

*Of all man's mechanical inventions, none has changed his way of living so drastically as the wheel. So great has been its impact that the technological progress of civilization can be measured in terms of the uses they have made of wheeled vehicles.*

(Time Inc. 1967)

Tire imprint investigators need to know the basic components of the tire, factors that must be considered in tire design, tread design variations, and how tread designs are developed.

## Basic Components of All Passenger Tires

All passenger tires share certain basic components, no matter what their construction. These components, shown in Figure 2.1, are:

*Beads:* As a tire rotates, the internal air pressure and centrifugal force tries to throw the tire off the rim. To prevent this, the plies of the tire are wrapped around bronze plated, high tensile steel wire, called beads. The beads anchor the tire to the rim, and are held in their proper place on the rim by air pressure within the tire.

*Cord body:* Layers of rubber coated cord, called plies, laid on top of one another and bonded together, make up the cord body of the tire. The cord body provides strength to the tire and acts as a container for the air pressure within the tire.

*Innerliner:* Bonded to the inside of the cord body, the innerliner retains air under pressure. It takes the place of a tube in a tubeless tire. The air supports the weight of the vehicle.

*Tread:* The portion of the tire in contact with the road surface is the tread.

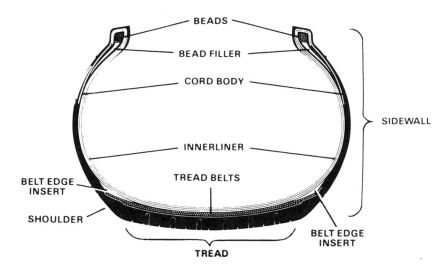

**Figure 2.1.** Passenger-tire cross section showing major components. (*Courtesy of Firestone Tire & Rubber Co.*)

Tread rubber is compounded to provide optimum wear, traction, and cut resistance.

*Sidewall:* The area from the bead to the tread is the sidewall. It forms a protective covering for the cord body. Side wall rubber is blended to resist cracking, cutting, and snagging.

*Belts:* Strong layers of cord under the tread area of a tire are known as stabilizer belts. They assist in improving tire mileage, impact resistance, and traction by giving the tread area extra strength and stability (Firestone 1982b).

The actual tread is normally composed of a blend of elastomers, unique to each manufacturer. If a sample of the rubber were obtained, it could be analyzed for a specific manufacturer.

*Footprint.* When a tire is deflected by load, it flattens until the ground-contact area multiplied by the inflation pressure approximately equals the load. The tire footprint, or contact patch on the road [Figure 2.2], is remarkable in its behavior. The tire footprint grips the road, steers the vehicle, and provides a comfortable and quiet ride. Tire engineering requires an extensive knowledge of the behavior of the stresses and movement, as well as noise generation and water flow within the contact patch. Continual advances in tread designs evolve to meet specific needs.

*Tread Pattern.* The tread pattern, or tread design, is a specialized area of tire engineering. The pattern usually consists of circumferential grooves and zigzag ribs. The ribs also normally contain sipes. Other tires may contain cross ribs or lugs. An unlimited number of designs is possible.

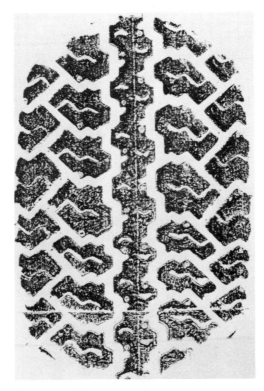

**Figure 2.2.**   Tire footprint. (*Courtesy of Firestone Tire & Rubber Co.*)

**Figure 2.3.**   Worn tread wear indicators. (*Courtesy of the Rubber Manufacturers Association*)

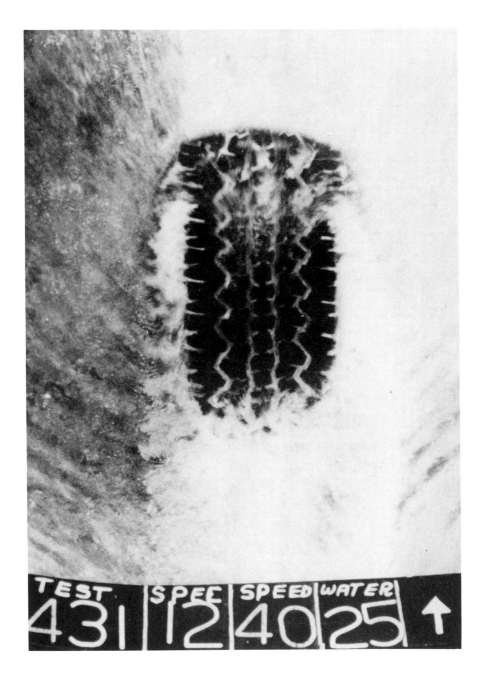

**Figure 2.4.** View below glass plate of heavy water film. (*Courtesy of Firestone Tire & Rubber Co.*)

The tread pattern on any tire provides adhesion (or grip) to the road, especially when wet. This is accomplished by wiping the road with the discrete design elements and channelling the water through the grooves and sipes. This squeegee action permits the tread rubber to grip the road surface.

If there is no pattern, water accumulates between the tread and the road, and traction and skid resistance are greatly reduced. This can sometimes lead to zero contact area, at which point the tire is completely supported on a film of water. Under these conditions, known as hydroplaning, the vehicle is difficult to control—a danger sometimes encountered when a car is operating on "bald" tires. For this reason, wear indicators are incorporated into the tread design; these are a series of radial bars that appear on the surface of the tire when the tread has been worn to 1/16 of an inch deep. Their appearance indicates that the tire should be replaced [Figure 2.3]. [Even a new tread pattern has difficulty cutting through a heavy water film on the road surface, see Figure 2.4.] The tread pattern also mechanically softens the tread, which permits better enveloping of small irregularities in the road surface (Kovac 1978).

The drawing board for today's tire designer is the computer screen. The designer creates a series of geometric shapes that vary in size to reduce road noise. A prediction of tire noise can be obtained and pitch sequences may be calculated (see Figure 2.5). Tire noise treatments are

**Figure 2.5.** Computer-generated pitch sequences. (*Courtesy of Firestone Tire & Rubber Co.*)

**Table 2.1.** Considerations for a New Tire Design

| Necessities | Performance | Appearance |
|---|---|---|
| Durability | Tread wear | Marketing objective |
| Ride | Traction | Styling |
| Handling | High speed | Customer requirements |
| Acceptable noise level | Power loss | |
| Marketing capabilities | Weight | |
| Cost-competitiveness | Riding comfort | |
| Construction | Uniformity | |

significant to the manufacturers and also to the investigators of tire impressions. This will be further discussed in Chapter 12.

Table 2.1 illustrates some of the many features that a tire designer must consider. The importance placed on each feature helps determine the new tire design appearance and purpose. Designers learn from each successive design and resultant tests, accounting for many very subtle changes.

# Tire Sales

3

*Americans make half-a-million car and truck tires daily. Standing side by side like lifesavers, they would stretch more than 50 miles. Americans also spend $250,000.00 a day getting rid of old tires. About 18 percent are retreaded, three percent are burned as fuel, and the rest end up in the landfills, creeks, or painted white with plants inside them.*

(Parker 1985)

The question of how many tires have been produced invariably becomes an issue in courtroom testimony. This chapter provides investigators and attorneys with an appreciation of the vast number of tire manufacturers, brands, tire designs, sizes, and cosmetic variations.

## The Global Tire Market

Worldwide demand during 1986 for all types of pneumatic tires was estimated in 1986 at more than 734 million units. Included in this total are 517 million automobile tires, 187 million truck tires, 22 million industrial and specialty tires, 7 million agricultural tires, 1 million aircraft tires, and an undetermined number of bicycle and motorcycle tires (Table 3.1). The investigator is usually interested only in passenger and truck tire identification.

Some 84 percent of the tires sold are manufactured by the ten largest tire manufacturers: Goodyear, Groupe Michelin, Bridgestone Corporation, Continental A.G., Firestone, Uniroyal Goodrich Tire Company, Pirelli Group, Sumitomo Rubber Industries Ltd., Yokohama Rubber Company Ltd., and Toyo Tire & Rubber Company Ltd. (*Rubber & Plastic News* 1987). Note that the names of tire manufacturers are also

**Table 3.1.** Worldwide Tire Demand, 1986 (millions of units)

| Country | Passenger | | | Truck | | |
|---|---|---|---|---|---|---|
| | Total | Replacement | O.E.[a] | Total | Replacement | O.E. |
| U.S. | 198 | 144 | 54 | 40 | 33 | 7 |
| Japan | 71 | 25 | 46 | 37 | 23 | 14 |
| West Germany | 39 | 20 | 19 | 4 | 2 | 2 |
| France | 28 | 17 | 11 | 3 | 2 | 1 |
| United Kingdom | 22 | 16 | 6 | 4 | 3 | 1 |
| Canada | 18 | 10 | 8 | 3 | 2 | 1 |
| Italy | 18 | 11 | 7 | 3 | 2 | 1 |
| Australia | 8 | 6 | 2 | 2 | 2 | 0 |
| Eastern Europe and China | 37 | 26 | 11 | 55 | 46 | 9 |
| South and Central America | 28 | 21 | 7 | 16 | 14 | 2 |
| Others | 50 | 34 | 16 | 20 | 16 | 4 |
| Worldwide total[b] | 517 | 330 | 187 | 187 | 145 | 42 |

*Source:* Courtesy of *Rubber & Plastic News* (1987).
[a] O.E. = original equipment.
[b] Plus an undetermined number of cycle tires.

constantly changing as a result of mergers and joint ventures. Investigators should also be cautious about limiting their attention to tire manufacturers in their own country. A significant number of tires are imported or exported throughout the world. Tires may enter any country on offshore manufactured vehicles or may be imported for the replacement market.

## Car and Truck Population

More than one-third of the estimated 381 million automobiles in use worldwide during 1986 were in the United States. Table 3.2 shows the countries with the largest number of automobiles. The world truck population is as follows. Of the world's 111.3 million trucks, North America has 42.8 million, Afro-Asia has 33.9 million, Western Europe has 14.0 million, Latin America has 7.4 million, and Eastern Europe and China have 13.2 million (*Rubber & Plastic News* 1987).

## Tread Designs

The investigator is likely to be overwhelmed by the more than 1,200 different passenger tire designs in the most recent *Tread Design Guide*. In addition to those, there are more than 1,100 different small highway

**Table 3.2.** Automobiles in Use Worldwide

| Country | No. of Automobiles (millions) |
|---|---|
| U.S. | 132.3 |
| Japan | 28.9 |
| West Germany | 26.5 |
| Italy | 22.9 |
| France | 21.6 |
| United Kingdom | 18.4 |
| U.S.S.R. | 13.1 |
| Canada | 10.7 |
| Brazil | 10.7 |
| Spain | 9.6 |
| Australia | 7.1 |
| Others | 79.2 |
| Total | 381.0 |

Source: Courtesy of Rubber & Plastics News (1987).

and light truck tire designs and more than 1,000 medium and large highway truck tire designs. However, some of these designs are duplications for different customers. (The publisher of the *Tread Design Guide* attempts to include pictures and descriptions of every tire design manufactured, but three distributors do not currently submit their tires: Shell Oil, Winston, and Vogue. The publisher of the *Guide* is making every effort to have 100 percent participation and to provide additional facts that may be useful to the investigator.)

To complicate identification further, a single tread design may be produced in a variety of sizes (shown in Figure 3.1). Furthermore, sometimes a design will have the option of three different cosmetic sidewalls: black, raised white stripe, and raised white letters.

## Questions to Ask the Tire Manufacturer's Sales Department

The investigator may want to check with the manufacturer's sales department for an estimate of the number of tires produced in a certain design.

If the size is identified, the question might be "How many tires of that design and size were produced in a year?"

If the size and the type of sidewall is identified, the question might be "How many tires of that design, size, and sidewall were produced in a year?"

If the size, type of sidewall, and specific mold feature (i.e., studs) are identified, the question might be "How many tires of that design, sidewall, and specific mold feature were produced in a year?"

## STEEL BELTED RADIAL 721

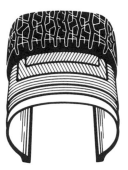

**Fabric body plies plus two steel belts under tread.**

| Tire Size | Load Range | Design Rim Width | New Tire Dimensions—Inches | | | |
|---|---|---|---|---|---|---|
| | | | Overall Tire Width | Overall Diameter | Static Loaded Radius | Tread Width |
| BR78-13 | B | 4.50 | 7.00 | 24.10 | 10.75 | 4.90 |
| BR78-14 | B | 4.50 | 6.80 | 24.60 | 11.05 | 4.76 |
| CR78-14 | B | 5.00 | 7.20 | 24.80 | 11.13 | 5.04 |
| DR78-14 | B | 5.00 | 7.40 | 25.20 | 11.28 | 5.18 |
| ER78-14 | B | 5.00 | 7.60 | 25.60 | 11.44 | 5.32 |
| FR78-14 | B | 5.50 | 8.05 | 26.10 | 11.63 | 5.64 |
| GR78-14 | B | 6.00 | 8.50 | 26.66 | 11.75 | 5.95 |
| HR78-14 | B,C | 6.00 | 8.80 | 27.36 | 12.01 | 6.16 |
| JR78-14 | B | 6.50 | 9.15 | 27.74 | 12.15 | 6.41 |
| GR78-15 | B | 6.00 | 8.35 | 27.32 | 12.20 | 5.85 |
| HR78-15 | B,D | 6.00 | 8.65 | 27.98 | 12.37 | 6.06 |
| JR78-15 | B | 6.50 | 9.05 | 28.34 | 12.50 | 6.34 |
| LR78-15 | B | 6.50 | 9.20 | 28.90 | 12.71 | 6.44 |
| BR70-13 | B | 5.50 | 7.60 | 24.10 | 10.75 | 5.32 |
| CR70-13 | B | 5.50 | 7.85 | 24.16 | 10.77 | 5.50 |
| DR70-14 | B | 5.50 | 7.90 | 25.24 | 11.30 | 5.53 |
| 195/70R13 | B | 5.50 | 7.85 | 24.16 | 10.77 | 5.50 |

**Figure 3.1.** A tread design may come in a variety of sizes. (*Courtesy of Firestone Tire & Rubber Co.*).

The next question might be "How many years has this tire design been in production?" or "Is this tire still in production?"

Additional questions might be "How is this tire distributed?" "Is this tire specifically made for O.E. [original equipment] or for trade sales [replacement tires] or both?" (Some O.E. tires are supplied for specific vehicles.)

The sales department may also be able to furnish the geographical sales distribution for a particular tire, and the manufacturer may have additional information about a specific design. Encourage any input the manufacturer can provide. For instance, the manufacturer might volunteer to make a tire registration check of people who purchased a certain type of tire.

**Table 3.3.** Useful Tire Manufacturer Directories

| Required | Optional |
|---|---|
| *Tread Design Guide* <br> *Who Makes It? and Where? Directory* | *The Tire Guide* <br> *Who Retreads Tires* <br> *Toll Free Digest* |

These directories can be obtained by writing to the following address: Tire Guides, 1101-6 South Rogers Circle, Boca Raton, FL 33487.

## Tire Manufacturer Directories

In addition to the annual editions of the *Tread Design Guide*, mentioned above, the *Who Makes It? and Where? Directory* lists all tire brand names and their manufacturer or distributor with toll-free telephone numbers. The *Consumer's Resource Handbook* may also help locate a manufacturer or distributor. Other useful Bennett Garfield publications are *The Tire Guide, Who Retreads Tires* and *The Toll Free Digest*.

An investigator does not need to purchase tire manufacturer directories, but he or she should know that they are available (see Table 3.3).

# Tires Have Distinctive Wear Patterns

# 4

*Treadwear is the useful life of a tire as determined by its wearing off due to abrasion on the road surface and depends on a multitude of factors.*

(Kovac 1978)

There is always an interaction between the vehicle and the tire. Abnormal tread wear can be traced back to the vehicle. In all my experience of investigating tires of suspects in crimes, I have found that some of the tire wear is due to vehicle irregularities.

## Improper Inflation Affects Wear

The Rubber Manufacturers Association (RMA) stresses that proper inflation is the most important requirement for maximum tire safety and mileage. Correct tire inflation provides proper sidewall deflection and a safe operating temperature for the tires. Underinflation creates excessive heat, lowers load-carrying capacity, can cause tire failure, uses extra gasoline, and seriously reduces tire life. However, studies show that vehicle owners seriously neglect maintaining proper air pressure: "Seventy percent of all cars are run with insufficient tyre pressures" (Bantle & Bott 1988). In fact, tire air pressure on a single vehicle often varies considerably from tire to tire. Investigators should note that this fact alone is a major reason that each tire develops distinctive "general accidental characteristics."

Furthermore, radial tires have a characteristic sidewall bulge that makes it impossible to see whether the tires are inflated properly merely by looking at them. In Figure 4.1, the tire on the right is

**Figure 4.1.** It is impossible to determine visually whether radial tires are properly inflated. (*Courtesy of Firestone Tire & Rubber Co.*)

underinflated by 33 percent. This means it will run hotter, wear faster and/or unevenly (adversely affecting vehicle handling), and possibly fail in service (RMA 1981).

## Causes and Effects of Abnormal Tread Wear

The Rubber Manufacturers Association (1987) gives the following causes of abnormal tread wear:

*Improper inflation.* Underinflation or overinflation causes uneven tread wear.

*Careless driving.* "Fast-cornering, jack-rabbit starts, sudden stops, excessive braking, riding edge of pavement, and high speeds all tend to wear away tread rubber rapidly."

*Rough road surface.* Rough road surfaces will wear tires more rapidly than smooth-surface roads.

*Squealing tires.* When tires slide or slip, they squeal. Factors that can induce tire squeal are "underinflation, speed, road surface, topography, temperature, and driving too fast on curves and around corners. The latter practice also causes abnormal wear in the

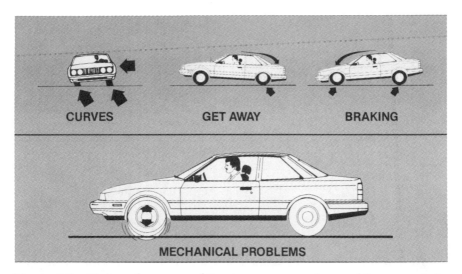

**Figure 4.2.** Various factors resulting in uneven tread wear. (*Courtesy of the Rubber Manufacturers Association*)

shoulder area of the tire. A tire's outside shoulder is particularly subject to wear as the vehicle negotiates sudden lane changes or cornering." (See Figure 4.2.)

*Unbalanced wheels.* Tire-wheel assemblies that are out of balance ruin tires and cause the vehicle to shake.

*Static imbalance* causes shaking from vertical vibration (Figure 4.3).

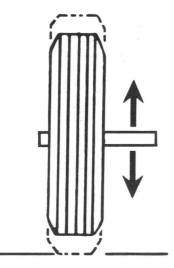

**Figure 4.3.** Static imbalance. (*Courtesy of the Rubber Manufacturers Association*)

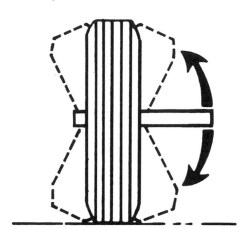

**Figure 4.4.** Dynamic imbalance. (*Courtesy of the Rubber Manufacturers Association*)

*Dynamic imbalance* causes wobble or shimmy from lateral vibration (Figure 4.4).

Imbalance of tires on a vehicle may be due to the mounting procedure or damage in operation.

*Mechanical irregularities.* "Misalignment of front or rear, improperly operating brakes or shock absorbers, bent wheels, sprung axle housings, worn bushings, etc., cause uneven and rapid tread wear." For example:

*Improper toe-in or toe-out* of the wheels causes excessive tread wear (Figure 4.5).

*Improper camber* (wheels tilted excessively inward or outward) causes more wear on one side of the tire (Figure 4.6).

*Faulty or "grabbing" brakes* can cause much the same conditions as out-of-balance wheels—flat spots and bald spots (Figure 4.7).

*Faulty or worn shock absorbers* cause irregular tire wear (Figure 4.8).

## Tire Rotation Patterns

Rotation of tires makes uniform wear for all tires on a vehicle possible. Figure 4.9 shows two popular types of rotation patterns. Either pattern is acceptable. Note that the special temporary spare is not to be included in the rotation. Fortunately for the investigator, rotation is generally neglected, which means that individual tire wear is more distinctive. The increased use of all-season designs is another reason that tires are rotated less often, because seasonal changes are not required.

**Figure 4.5.** Improper toe-in or toe-out causing excessive tread wear. (*Courtesy of the Rubber Manufacturers Association*)

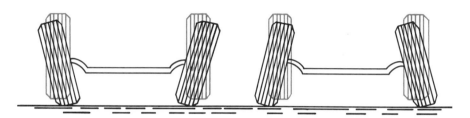

**Figure 4.6.** Improper camber causing wear on one side of the tire. (*Courtesy of the Rubber Manufacturers Association*)

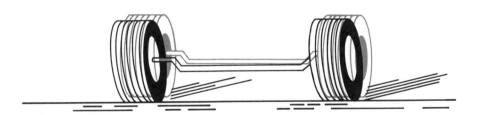

**Figure 4.7.** Faulty or "grabbing" brakes causing flat spots and bald spots. (*Courtesy of the Rubber Manufacturers Association*)

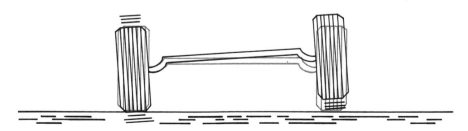

**Figure 4.8.** Faulty or worn shock absorbers causing irregular tire wear. (*Courtesy of the Rubber Manufacturers Association*)

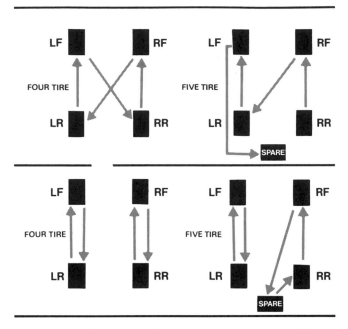

**Figure 4.9.** Two popular types of tire rotation patterns. (*Courtesy of the Rubber Manufacturers Association*)

## Sidewall Wear

A very common sidewall condition is caused by the tire abrading against the curb. The abrasion is often so severe that white rubber is exposed through the thin black covering veneer on white sidewalls. This abrasion may help determine the tires' position. White sidewalls are generally mounted facing outward, and front right tire sidewalls are subjected to more abuse than rears.

# Sidewalls

5

*Sidewall details are very commonly found on clothing, indeed on occasions they are the only tyre marks found.*

(Grogan 1971)

White sidewalls predominate in North America, but the styling trend is toward black sidewalls—the "European look." This is a very positive direction for tire engineers, because decorative sidewalls perform no useful function. Now the attention is being focused on attractive wheels to compliment black sidewalls.

Sidewall variations abound, and the cosmetic appearance of tire sidewalls can be more obvious from a distance than the tire tread design. For this reason, noting the tire sidewall may be a good way to rapidly sort out tires on many vehicles.

Typically the *Tread Design Guides* only shows pictures of one type of sidewall for a particular design. Figures 5.1–5.4 show all the typical styles of sidewalls. Additional combinations of decorative sidewall variations may be used as shown in Figures 5.5–5.8. Decorative "portawalls" that can be mounted to cover a tire's sidewall are available too, as are special ground and painted sidewalls. White sidewall tires can also be mounted with the black side out. Fortunately these variations are not common, which makes it easier for the investigator. Check with the manufacturer for currently available sidewall variations.

Case Study 5.1 shows how sidewall design can be crucial in tire identification and how important it is to take the sidewalls into consideration.

**Figure 5.1.** Blackwall (B). (*Courtesy of Firestone Tire & Rubber Co.*)

**Figure 5.2.** Whitewall (W). (*Courtesy of Firestone Tire & Rubber Co.*)

**Figure 5.3.** White Letters (WL). (*Courtesy of Firestone Tire & Rubber Co.*)

**Figure 5.4.** Outline white letters (OWL). (*Courtesy of Firestone Tire & Rubber Co.*)

### *Case Study 5.1.*

In 1983 the *Chicago Lawyer*, a monthly publication, asked me to help the review of a previously tried homicide. A tire imprint had been involved in the conviction.

I reviewed the actual plaster casting (Figure 5.9) and found that it had clearly been made from a tire *similar to*, but not the same as, a Uniroyal PR 6 (Figure 5.10), as described by some investigator in

**Figure 5.5.** Decorative sidewall. (*Courtesy of Firestone Tire & Rubber Co.*)

**Figure 5.6.** Wide white sidewall. (*Courtesy of Firestone Tire & Rubber Co.*)

**Figure 5.7.** Combination of stripe and letters. (*Courtesy of Firestone Tire & Rubber Co.*)

**Figure 5.8.** Recessed black letters. (*Courtesy of Uniroyal Goodrich Tire Co.*)

the trial. This was a trial for murder and a conviction was made. (The PR 6 has a decoupling groove in the shoulder and does not wear into a solid wide rib with sipes, as highlighted with arrows in Figure 5.9.) The casting was of a tire design that was unique and yet extremely general in the tread design.

**Figure 5.9.** Plaster cast of 1983 crime scene imprint. Arrows show solid wide rib. (*Courtesy of* Chicago Lawyer)

In the early 1970s, Firestone had designed a radial tire for General Motors (GM) that was later referred to as the TPC (Tire Performance Criteria). For many years, but fortunately no longer, GM required all its manufacturers to furnish tires with the identical tread pattern, so it was nearly impossible to distinguish between a TPC tire tread made by, for instance, Goodyear or Uniroyal or Firestone. In addition, the many duplicates or variations of this "standard" made identification even more difficult. However, the sidewall did display the manufacturer's name.

**Figure 5.10.** Test imprint of Uniroyal PR 6 steel-belted radial GR 78-15 shows a decoupling groove defining the shoulder rib.

The tire in this case was indistinguishable to me in the tread area, but the upper sidewall (Figure 5.9, highlighted with arrows) was unique. The faint sidewall sipes show a variation difference that does not occur in a Uniroyal PR 6.

## How to Read Tire Size Designations on Sidewalls

Tire manufacturers use several systems of tire size designation. They include the "P metric" system, the alphanumeric system, the metric system, and the numeric system.

### The "P Metric" System

The "P metric" system, which is based on international standards, is the newest type of tire size identification. In this system, each component involved in tire size identification may vary, depending on the tire's section width, height-to-width ratio, construction, and rim diameter. The first letter (P) identifies the tire as a passenger car tire. The first number is the section width (in millimeters). The second number is the section height-to-width ratio, and so on (see Table 5.1).

### The Alphanumeric System

In the alphanumeric size designation (Table 5.2), the first letter designates the load-carrying capability and size of the tire. The lower the letter, the smaller the size and load-carrying capability of a tire at a given inflation pressure. The next letter, R, indicates that the tire is of radial construction. The first number indicates the tire's approximate section height-to-width ratio (in the table, "78" means that the tire section is 78 percent as high as it is wide). The last number indicates

**Table 5.1.** The "P Metric" Tire-Size Identification System

| P | 195/ | 75 | R | 14 |
|---|---|---|---|---|
| Identifies tire as a passenger car tire | Section width in millimeters | Section height-to-width ratio | Identifies tire construction: *R* if radial; *B* if belted bias; *D* if diagonal (bias) | Rim diameter in inches |

*Source:* From the Rubber Manufacturers Association (1987).

**Table 5.2.** The Alphanumeric Tire-Size Identification System

| E | R | 78- | 14 |
|---|---|-----|-----|
| Identifies load/size | Radial | Section height-to-width ratio | Rim diameter in inches |

*Source:* From the Rubber Manufacturers Association (1987).

the nominal rim size in inches ("14" indicates that the tire fits a 14-inch rim). For tires that are not radial construction, the "R" is omitted.

## The Metric System

The metric size-designation system uses a three-digit number (195) to indicate the approximate cross-section width in millimeters, followed by "R" for radial, and "14" for the rim diameter in inches. Thus the size designation "195 R 14," for example, would mean that the approximate cross-section width is 195 millimeters, the tire is a radial tire, and the rim diameter is 14 inches. This system is sometimes referred to as "European metric," because it originated in Europe.

## The Numeric System

The numeric size-designation system is the oldest system and is still found on some tires today. In the designation "6.45-14," for instance, the first number (6.45) refers to the approximate cross-section width of an inflated tire in inches, and the second number (14) is the rim diameter in inches.

## The Sidewall Story

The Rubber Manufacturers Association (1987) provides the following rundown of the tire size information given on tire sidewalls, as shown in the example in Figure 5.11:

"P195/75R14": A current size marking for a popular "P metric" radial tire.

"Radial": Designates a tire of radial construction. All such tires must have the word "radial" on the sidewall.

"Standard (or Extra) Load": Identifies the load and inflation limits for a given size tire when used under certain conditions. The only other current such designation used is "Extra Load." Prior to the use of these

**Figure 5.11.** Typical sidewall stamping. (*Courtesy of Rubber Manufacturers Association*)

designations, load limits were identified with the term "load range" and, before that, "ply rating."

"Max. Load 635 kg (1400 lbs.) @ 240 kPa (35 psi) maximum pressure": Indicates the tire's load limits and maximum *cold* inflation. These "P metric" tire sidewall markings are given in both metric and English terms. (For normal operation, follow the pressure recommendations in the owner's manual or on the vehicle tire information placard.)

"4 plies under tread (2 xxxx cord + 2 xxxx cord), Sidewall 2 plies xxxx cord": Indicates tire ply composition and material used.

"DOT xxxx xxxxxx": The letters "DOT" certify compliance with Department of Transportation tire safety standards. Adjacent to this is a tire identification or serial number (see below). The first characters identify the tire manufacturer; the remaining characters identify the tire size, type, and date of manufacture.

"Tubeless": The tire must be marked either "tubeless" or "tube-type."

"M/S": Any combination of the letters M and S indicates that the tires meet the Rubber Manufacturers Association definition for a mud and snow tire.

## The Tire Identification or Serial Number

The tire serial number appears on the back sidewall near the bead. This combination of letters and numbers is used by all tire manufacturers. For example, the serial number "DOT W2 L8 L0K 216" provides the following information.

DOT  Tire meets or exceeds minimum safety standards set by the U.S. Department of Transportation.

W2  Code combination given by the Department of Transportation to each tire manufacturing plant.

L8  The manufacturer's code indicating tire size.

L0K  The manufacturer's code of up to four symbols to identify significant design characteristics of the tire.

216  Three numbers are used to identify the week and year the tire was produced. The first two digits denote the week; the last digit denotes the year of manufacture. In the example here, "216" denotes the twenty-first week of 1986.

*Note:* Listing tire serial numbers is one way to record tires, but if tires of the same brand and same week of manufacture are being recorded, the examiner should indicate the mold number and/or mark additional reference numbers on all tires with a crayon. These mold numbers can generally be found on the back side near the rim.

## Sidewall Variations

Tire mold sidewalls are generally hand-stamped (see Figure 5.12). Small stamps are hand-held in position and pounded in to the desired depth by a large hammer. Therefore, some inconsistency in depth may

**Figure 5.12.**  Inside of mold showing hand-stamping. (*Courtesy of Firestone Tire & Rubber Co.*)

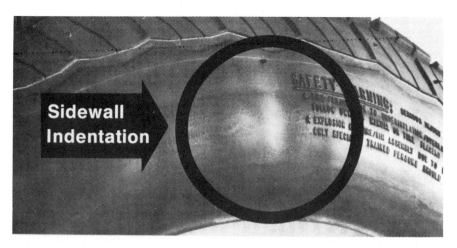

**Figure 5.13.** Sidewall indentation. (*Courtesy of the Rubber Manufacturers Association*)

be visible. Sidewall stampings are generally located on a separate part of the mold from the tread ring. Therefore, the stamping location on one mold may not align with the tread in exactly the same circumferential orientation as another mold.

Tire side treatment configurations may occur in deep impressions or on the clothing of a victim. Even a small impression could provide valuable information.

According to the Rubber Manufacturers Association (1987), "radial tire sidewalls have indentations or anomalies that are in a unique position for each tire produced. The indentations are common to radial tires and do not affect the performance of the tire. Radial tire body ply cords run straight across the tire from bead to bead. Because of this construction, the joining of the ply material in the sidewall area may sometimes cause a slight indentation or wavy appearance on the sidewall surface of the inflated tire" (see Figure 5.13).

Tire retail sales outlets owned by the tire manufacturers are required to register the name and address of purchasers along with tire identification or serial numbers. Such records can sometimes help track down a car owner. This is something to keep in mind if an imprint was made by a replacement tire. If a known criminal's name appears on a list of purchasers of a specific tire design and size it would be a logical lead to pursue. In a homicide case in Monterey, California, I identified an imprint of a N50-15 Parnelli Jones tire manufactured by Firestone. Firestone made a registration check, and the name of the murderer came up on the computer printout. (See Case Study 10.5 in Chapter 10.)

# The Crime Scene

6

*A motor vehicle is used in 75 percent of all the major crimes reported today.*

(Given, Nehrich, and Shields 1977)

Even though as many as 75 percent of major crimes involve an automobile (see quotation above), investigators do not appear to be seriously looking for and recording tire-imprint evidence at the scene of the crime. Investigators need to be more aware of the importance of making a thorough search for tire imprints at the crime scene, and of the procedures for recording such evidence. *Forensic tire investigation is probably the most commonly available and effective method of arriving at a positive identification of a vehicle at a crime scene.*

## Isolation and Protection of the Scene

The first officer at the crime scene should assess and attempt to determine the entire area of the crime scene, including paths of entry and exit and any areas that may include evidence. Unfortunately, tire tracks are often easily eradicated by weather or by people and vehicles approaching the scene from the same direction of entry or escape. Isolation of the area and protection of the scene is crucial, so that having to analyze all those recently made police car tire tracks can be avoided.

## Methods of Recording Tire Impression Evidence

There are four basic methods of recording tire impression evidence at the crime scene. One or all may be used.

**Figure 6.1.** Plastic print in mud is well defined.

1. Photography
2. Castings
3. Liftings
4. Wheelbase and tire tread stance measurements

The investigator should "use known methods in the best possible way to develop evidence to its fullest potential" (Cassidy 1980).

## Tire Imprints

Tire imprints may be divided into four separate categories: plastic prints, positive visible prints, negative visible prints, and latent prints.

### Plastic Prints

Plastic tire imprints are impressions that occur when the tire tread rolls over a soft pliable surface, such as deep mud or snow, wet sand, tar, or even the body of the victim (see Figures 6.1 and 6.2). This produces a negative impression of the tread element, resulting in a plastic print. In a dry winter condition, the enduring signature of a tire track compressed into snow can remain in relief even after the winds erase softer drifts around the print.

**Figure 6.2.** Plastic print on girl's forehead. (*Courtesy of Brown, Todd, Hagood & Davenport, Attorneys-at-Law*)

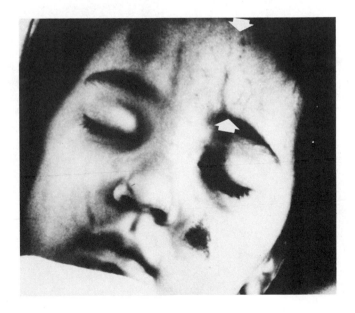

## Positive Visible Prints

Positive visible tire prints occur when the tire tread rolls over a foreign substance and is contaminated by it, and then comes in contact with a clean surface and is pressed onto that surface. Such positive visible prints can even be found on a victim's clothing. The most common positive type is the mud print left on the contrasting blacktop road surface (see Figure 6.3). When a warm, loaded tire is rolled over an icy surface, a positive image is often transferred. A variety of other substances, such as blood, grease, or oil, may leave a contrasting positive imprint. Figure 6.4 shows an imprint made from a suspect's tire that had gone through a puddle of the victim's blood and then onto the clean road surface.

## Negative Visible Prints

Negative visible tire imprints occur when a tire tread rolls over a thin film of dust, water, oil, snow, or the like, and actually lifts that substance, laying a negative imprint on the clean road surface next.

**Figure 6.3.** Positive visible print left by tire that rolled from muddy shoulder onto contrasting blacktop surface. (*Courtesy of New Jersey Division of Criminal Justice*)

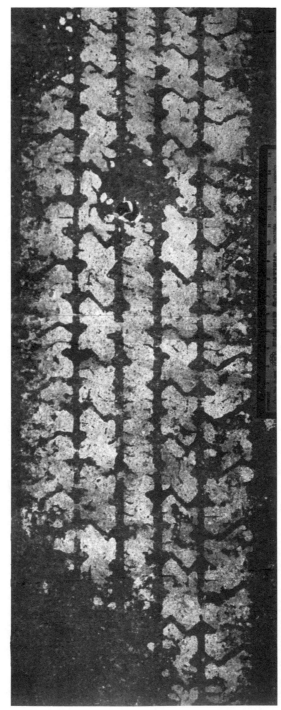

**Figure 6.4.** Positive visible print from tire that rolled through blood, then onto a clean road surface. (*Courtesy of The Winnipeg Crown Attorney's Office*)

## Latent Prints

Latent prints, which are unfortunately largely overlooked, are generally found on a smooth surface. They can be developed the same way fingerprints or shoe prints are. I have never prepared a latent tire imprint, but Corporal L. A. Nause (1987), of the Royal Canadian Mounted Police describes an experiment with latent prints:

> [A] tire was mounted on a vehicle and driven over paved roads and then parked in a paved parking lot with no other special attention given to it. The vehicle was then driven over a piece of cardboard box [Figure 6.5]. The exhibit was then recovered. If the direction of travel and tire location is known for the vehicle, it should be marked on the exhibit. In this case, from evidence at the scene, if I knew it was the right rear tire that had made the impression I would mark it as such. As well, if direction of travel can be determined I place an arrow on the exhibit or in the photograph pointing to the front of the vehicle. This arrow acts like the laterality letter *R* in fingerprint photography. Most tread designs are nondirectional and when reversed will appear the same, since one half of the tread design is like a mirror image of the other. By having the arrow in the photograph or on the exhibit, you will always know which is the inside and outside edge of the tire impression. Marking the impression by placing the letters *RR* or designation of tire position will also help

**Figure 6.5.** Latent print from cardboard box. (*Courtesy of L. A. Nause, RCMP*)

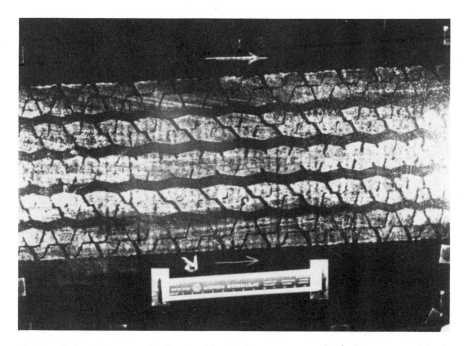

**Figure 6.6.** Photograph obtained by carbon paper method. (*Courtesy of L. A. Nause, RCMP*)

maintain laterality in the darkroom, but this is over and above some method of marking for inside and outside edge of the impression, if that fact is known.

This type of impression [a latent print] is not easily observed since it is light colored on a light surface. It can be seen from an oblique angle [but] it is difficult to photograph. Using a technique which is well known in footwear identification, the dust impression was lifted using the carbon paper method. This involves securing the exhibit from moving and covering it with a 14″ × 17″ sheet of carbon paper. The carbon paper is then held from slipping while it is stroked with a piece of fur or like substance to create static. The carbon paper was then removed and contained a reversed lift of the dust impression. The arrow to maintain direction to the front of the vehicle was transferred to the carbon paper using a grease marker. A reversed letter R was then marked on the carbon paper so when a photograph was made the R could be printed laterally correct making the impression laterally correct as well. The carbon paper was then stretched over a piece of mounting board and illuminated with oblique lighting. [The photograph obtained is shown in Figure 6.6.]

Another test case, prepared by Stephen Ojena with Kinderprint Company, is displayed in Figures 6.7 and 6.8. A piece of cardboard (Figure 6.7) was run over by a dusty tire, but the imprint is totally invisible.

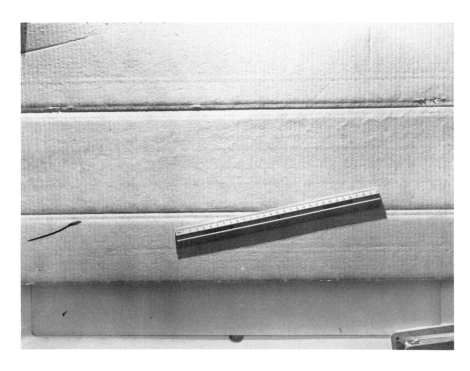

**Figure 6.7.** Latent tire imprint on cardboard in Ojena test. (*Courtesy of Stephen Ojena, Kinderprint Co., Inc.*)

**Figure 6.8.** Electrostatically lifted dust print from cardboard in Ojena test. (*Courtesy of Steven Ojena, Kinderprint Co., Inc.*)

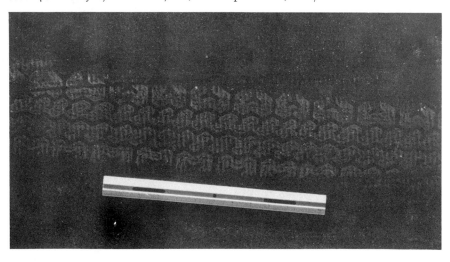

The same piece of cardboard was then lifted electrostatically, and the results are clearly visible in Figure 6.8.

## General Crime Scene Photographs

Tire imprints are generally found outdoors. The locations that will later be photographed in detail should be photographed showing the general crime scene and surrounding area. Always give a relationship to a known object in the scene. (Scale in photographs is described in greater detail in Chapter 7.) Take pictures at eye level to show exactly how the scene appeared to the investigator. Include photo evidence numbers in the photograph to help key the location of imprints.

## Admissibility of Photographic Evidence

The investigator or photographer should understand the techniques and legal requirements necessary to ensure that the crime scene photographs will be admissible in court. The basic premise involved in crime scene photography is that the photographs are a true representation of the scene as it was at the time the incident was reported. Photograph the scene before detailed photos of specific imprints are taken with an added scale and a description card in the picture.

I testified in a case in which I was able to make a positive identification, connecting the suspect's tire impression with one of many photos taken at a homicide crime scene. Unfortunately, the individual imprints were random and the photographer did not have good overall scene photographs. In addition, the photographer's memory of the scene was also clouded when testifying. This did not help my testimony, which was based entirely on photographed imprints.

## The Crime Scene Drawing

Some crime scenes, particularly those involving tire tracks in a widely scattered area, require more than an overall scene photograph. A drawing of the crime scene brings out one more dimension that will assist the court, witnesses, and yourself possibly months or even years later. This crime scene drawing may be keyed with photographic evidence numbers that locate the photographed imprints. If possible, designate tire position, show tire direction of travel, make reference to known objects and include the North arrow and as many other pertinent facts as possible. Always list case number and location, and date and sign the drawing.

# Recording Tire Imprints

# 7

*The observation "A picture is worth a thousand words," credited to Confucius, is not quite accurate. What he did write, "One seeing is worth a thousand tellings," differs considerably. Consider also the definition of a "photograph." The word comes from two Greek words: "phos," which means "light," and "graph," meaning "to write." Therefore, the technical definition of a photograph is "writing with light."*

(Fletcher 1985)

Photographs taken at the crime scene can help make a positive identification. They can be used to help discover what kind of vehicle may have been used in a crime, or they may be used to compare with a suspect's tires for a possible positive identification. This chapter covers the procedure for photographing and casting tire imprints at the scene of a crime.

## Photographs vs. Castings

Photography, which is two-dimensional is the method I prefer for recording most tire imprints. The other method would be casting, which is three-dimensional. The appearance of most tire patterns changes with wear, which allows the investigator to establish the approximate third dimension (depth) in a photograph. If a fine blade of grass, pebble, or foreign object were recorded only in a casting, there could be some question about whether it was an accidental characteristic made by the tire or a characteristic of the casting. Likewise, a void in the casting can be confusing. I have made positive identifications with many good tire castings, but if I had to choose between castings

**Figure 7.1.** Photograph of a tire imprint in a granular surface. (*Courtesy of Robert J. Link, Attorney and Counselor-at-Law*)

and photographs, I prefer photographs. Photographs of tire imprints in a granular surface are far superior to casts of such imprints. Compare the same imprint in Figure 7.1 (a photograph) and Figure 7.2 (a casting). Fortunately the photograph was taken in advance. The casting was of no value at all.

## Castings

Castings are much more limiting than photographs. First, when castings are made only a short section can be cast easily. For this reason, the examiner determines the most valuable portion of the imprint to record and in doing so may obscure an important adjacent section. Footwear imprints, by contrast, are short and more adaptable for establishing casting limits. Tire tracks are generally long and less defined in length.

Second, while an imprint on an incline is difficult to cast, the camera may be easily inclined perpendicular to the imprint.

Third, a photograph of an imprint can be compared directly with a test impression, but to develop a negative imprint to be compared directly with the negative test impression, it is necessary to photograph the positive casting. This adds an extra step. Remember always

**Figure 7.2.** Casting of a tire imprint in a granular surface. (*Courtesy of Robert J. Link, Attorney and Counselor-at-Law*)

to include a scale in a photograph of the casting. (Do not try comparing the casting directly with a suspect's tire. That would be comparing a loaded tire imprint with an unloaded one. In addition, the two cannot be overlayed for direct comparison.

Special Agent William Bodziak (1987) of the Federal Bureau of Investigation offers the following comparison of photography and casting to show how they "enhance one another to give the examiner the best possible evidence."

*Photography*

Backs up casting.

Shows impression as it was at scene.

Shows detail of impression and debris in and around the impression to correlate with cast if necessary.

In some instances, such as with impression in coarse sand or gravel impressions, photographs may show more.

*Casting*

Gives tangible evidence to jury (3-D).

Gives life-like molding of the actual impression, including uneven surface.

No focus problem.

No scale problem.

Backs up photography if photos fail.

If castings *are* prepared, photographs of any areas to be cast should be taken *before* the casting. After imprints are thoroughly photographed the experienced examiner should make a casting. Some of the techniques described by Michael Cassidy in his book *Footwear Identification* will be applicable (see Cassidy 1980). Surface, temperature, and experience are factors in determining what casting material to use.

## How to Make One Type of a Tire Casting

Class 1 dental stone is the best material for casting tire imprints in mud, sand, or soft soil. Most dental laboratory suppliers furnish this material, listed under different trade names.

If dental stone is needed in a hurry and has not been ordered in advance, I would suggest asking your local dentist for assistance. The cost is approximately one dollar per pound in twenty-five pound containers. The material needed to cast a tire impression includes:

Dental stone

Water

Bucket

Stirring stick

Marking pen

### *Procedure for Preparing the Casting*

Pour approximately twenty-four ounces of water into the bucket (two 12-ounce beverage cans may be a convenient measure). Then pour five pounds of dental stone into the bucket, allowing it to "cone-up" in the center. Allow to stand one or two minutes. Then stir until the dental stone is completely dissolved. Stir often until the consistency is similar to pancake batter, about eight to ten minutes. Pour the mixture into the tire imprint, slowly down the stirring stick holding it to the side of the imprint so as not to damage the fragile raised elements. No forming will be necessary if prepared to the proper consistency and if the cast is in a generally level area. Dental stone is very strong, requiring only one-half inch thickness above the tread elements. And no reinforcing is needed. It is not practical to cast more than two feet in length.

The investigator should mark the back of the casting with identification notations. These notations are later described under "Making the Imprint Identification Card." In future examinations it may be necessary to correlate a photograph location with a casting location.

The casting should set up in about 30 minutes. Then carefully lift the casting from the imprint but do not try to clean off material that may be adhering to it. Let air dry for approximately one day and then wash off debris with a water spray. Never wrap in airtight container or plastic; the cast will contain moisture.

## Which Tire Imprints to Photograph?

Photographs are first taken of the general tire track scene, and specific locations are identified (see Chapter 6). The next step is to photograph each tire imprint in detail. Remember, film is cheap. Don't limit the number of photographs—you'll probably not have another chance, and most tire imprints are very fragile.

Even a partial imprint may be very important evidence. Because tires are generally symmetrical, even half the tread width may make identification possible. Even a long single rib impression can help establish a sequence of tread elements in the total circumference. As few as three pitches in half the tread width may be satisfactory for establishing an exact location on a suspect's test impression (see Chapter 12 and Figure 12.5). Even if there is doubt about the significance of a single tire imprint, take a photograph. A few inches of a good imprint may make an identification.

## Taking Admissible Photographs

Before specific tire imprints are photographed the general area of the imprints should be photographed. The relationship of the imprints to some known landmark is important to establish the scene for future testimony. These first undisturbed photos are an opportunity to practice tripod positions, framing the imprint, focus and exposure setting, flash angle, and the location of the shield to block out direct sunlight.

Remember: Use no scales, ID cards, or markers before taking a general scene or close-up photograph of the tire imprints, and don't clean up the imprint initially. If additional markers are shown in the picture, the defense counsel can argue that the tire imprint has been altered and is not the same as when it was discovered. After the general scene and close-up photographs are taken, the scale and ID card for each imprint to be photographed can be added. All tire imprint photographs should be on their own rolls of film to avoid confusion with other evidence.

## Preparing the Impression

After making the initial photograph or photographs, remove any foreign objects that may have collected in the impression since it was originally made. Remove larger objects with tweezers; blow out smaller objects with an ear syringe. Small bits of dirt and debris can generally be removed by dampening a long-handled cotton swab with oil and carefully touching the object.

Impressions in snow frequently will be damaged by drifting snow or by a fresh snowfall. A compressed-air can (used to blow away dust in a darkroom) can restore them to their original state. "Before blasting the impression with air, try it out in the immediate surrounding area first to determine how close you should start. Remember, in most cases, you are starting out with very little evidence, so you have everything to gain. It would be wise to practice before using this method at a crime scene. Be sure not to shake or tip the new can too much, as propellent may be expelled which may damage the fragile print" (Cassidy 1980).

## Making the Imprint Identification Card

Prepare a 3-by-5 card for each imprint to be photographed. This card may have some of the following information boldly displayed:

Investigator's name

Date / time

Case number

Key number from sketch (update sketch key as imprints are photographed)

Define location of imprint with compass direction (North arrow) or reference point

Outside of tire (if known)

Position of tire (if known)

Direction of travel (if known)

The direction of travel may be determined by many factors: overlapping tire imprints, damp soil or puddled liquid lifted in direction of travel, direction of flattened vegetation, direction of residue from spinning tire, material transferred from one area to another, indication of vehicle maneuvers. Place the identification card next to the imprint so it will appear in the picture. Take care not to cover a portion of the tire imprint.

## Use of the Flash Attachment and Oblique Lighting

The flash attachment is very important in photographing tire imprints. The flash should be used for each picture of a tire imprint. It should not be installed on the camera, but extended from the camera with a five-foot sync cord, as shown in Figure 7.3.

Held at approximately a 45-degree angle, the flash will throw shadows from all tread features. These shadows help give definition and depth to the two-dimensional photograph. Imprints are usually photographed in the daylight. If the imprint is in direct sunlight, the photographer should shield the area involved so that the flash will throw the effective shadows. The photographer's body may throw all the shadow necessary for a tire imprint (see Figure 7.3). In case a shadow obscures some significant detail, a *second* picture should always be taken with the flash held at a 180-degree angle from the first picture.

**Figure 7.3.** Body sun shield and sync cord. (*Courtesy of Gary Truszkowski, Michigan State Police*)

**Figure 7.4.** Cardboard sun shield and self-timer. (*Courtesy of Gary Truszkowski, Michigan State Police*)

Ideally, the flash should be held at both sides of the tire imprint, plus at the front and rear for each imprint. If a tripod is not used an assistant must hold the flash. A very faint imprint—for example, dust—will require that the flash be almost at the imprint level for enhancement. If the self-timer is used, the shutter release cable is not necessary and will free the photographer's hands to hold the flash and sun shield (see Figure 7.4).

Sergeant Gary Truszkowski of the Michigan State Police has written an excellent paper titled "Daylight Flash Photography of Three-Dimensional Impressions." Film speed, flash angle, and distance from the impression are factors considered. It is the most complete study I know, and I recommend it for your reading if you desire more precise information.

## Reference Scales

Reference scales are important in scientific photography. W. G. Hyzer, a noted expert in forensic photogrammetry, states: "An inaccurate or poorly placed scale can seriously diminish the intrinsic value of an otherwise sound scientific record" (Hyzer 1986). I have examined tire imprint photographs with a variety of reference scales, and some with none at all. The most common scales are shown in Figure 7.5, items 1, 2, and 3. These scales have generally been satisfactory for my purposes, but each has its drawbacks. There are more effective systems to add a reference scale to tire imprint photographs without complication, as shown in items 4, 5, and 6 in Figure 7.5. (Practice photographing tire impressions. Try your old system of scale and then make your own comparison.) A linear scale is often satisfactory, but a circular scale has many advantages that are further described.

According to Hyzer, "any linear dimension of known units serves as a means of measuring the size of an object as long as the object and the scale fall in the same object plane, and the required spatial measurement is taken along the scale's axial direction" (Hyzer 1981). On the subject of reference scales, Hyzer (1981) advises:

> A simple linear scale running horizontally through the field of view, for example, may not provide accurate vertical measurements if the camera is tilted either up or down. Likewise, a single scale of measurement in the field of view is not usually sufficient to measure objects that fall outside of the scale's plane of focus. The only time that I routinely use a linear scale is in photomacography, where the depth of field is shallow enough

**Figure 7.5.**   Scales for photographing tire imprints.

| TYPES OF SCALES | AVAILABILITY | ACCURACY (DEPRESSED SURFACE) | ACCURACY (FLAT SURFACE) | MAINTAIN VIEW OF EVIDENCE | INDICATION OF CAMERA TILT | THIRD DIMENSION POTENTIAL (3-D) | NEED TO RETAIN FOR DIMENSIONS | FLASH HGT. & ANGLE (FOR RECONSTRUCTION) |
|---|---|---|---|---|---|---|---|---|
| 1. REFERENCE OBJECTS (PEN, FLASHLIGHT, ETC.) | GOOD | POOR | FAIR | FAIR | POOR | POOR | YES | NO |
| 2. LINEAR (SHORT RULER) | FAIR | POOR | GOOD | FAIR | POOR | POOR | NO | NO |
| 3. "L" SHAPE (CARPENTER'S SQ., 90° TYPE | POOR | POOR | GOOD | POOR | GOOD | POOR | NO | NO |
| 4. CIRCULAR (DISC OF KNOWN DIA., COIN) | GOOD | GOOD | GOOD | GOOD | GOOD | POOR | NO | NO |
| 5. GOLF BALL SPOTTERS (SPIKE STICKING UP) | FAIR | GOOD | GOOD | GOOD | GOOD | GOOD | YES | YES |
| 6. STANDARD BALL SPOTTERS (SUPPLIED TO ALL) | GOOD | GOOD | GOOD | GOOD | GOOD | GOOD | NO | YES |

so that from a practical stand point, all measurements are made within essentially the same plane through the object.

I find that a circular scale is much more practical than a linear scale for many other routine applications involving three-dimensional scenes that may require quantitative reconstruction from their photographic images. By a circular scale, I mean an inscribed circle or a flat disc of known diameter.

It is important in using any of these scales that the actual diameter of the circle be legibly printed in the "center of the circle" or retained or if it is a coin, its denomination should be discernable. (A coin is generally available, small and easy to insert into the tread surface plane.) This avoids ambiguities that may arise later concerning the size of the scale used. The size and boldness of the numeral should be sufficient to be clearly visible in the photographic image. Why do I prefer a circle as a scale of reference in a photograph? For two reasons:

1. The plane of the circle does not have to be aligned parallel to the plane of the film in order to provide a quantitatively useful scale of reference.
2. The distorted shape of a circle when it is viewed obliquely is indicative of the viewing angle. (Hyzer 1986)

Figure 7.6 demonstrates angle $\theta$ from the perpendicular. Figure 7.7

**Figure 7.6.** Angle $\theta$ from the perpendicular. (*Courtesy of W. G. Hyzer, forensic photogrammetry expert*)

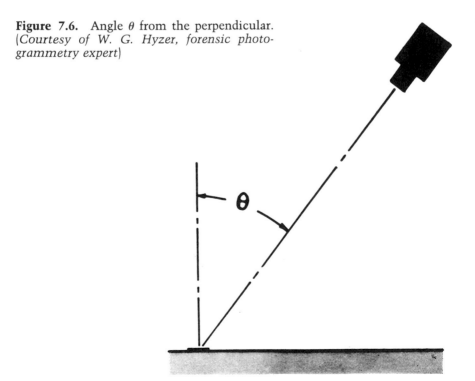

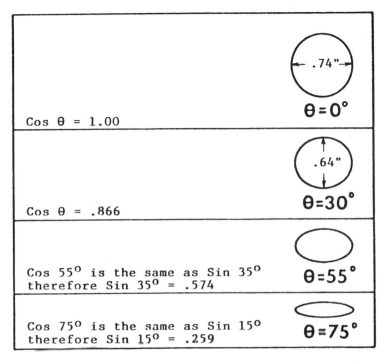

**Figure 7.7.** Circle viewed at different angles.

pictures a circle viewed at different angles, called $\theta$. The formula for determining the angle $\theta$ of obliquity is:

$$\cos \Theta = \frac{N}{M} \qquad \begin{array}{l} N = \text{minor axis} \\ M = \text{major axis} \end{array}$$

Example: Circle in Figure 7.7 has a 0.74″ diameter. If the circle is photographed at an angle, it becomes an ellipse. If the minor axis ($N$) is 0.64″ and the major axis ($M$) remains 0.74″, $\theta$ can be calculated:

$$\frac{0.64}{0.74} = 0.865 = \cos \Theta$$

A basic trigonometry table tells us that angle $\theta$ is approximately equal to 30 degrees. As an outgrowth of the circular scale principle I began using an additional vertical (three-dimensional) scale. (As children we learned that the height of a tree could be measured by measuring the length of its shadow. This was done by comparing a known height and its measured shadow length. A formula could be used to determine the

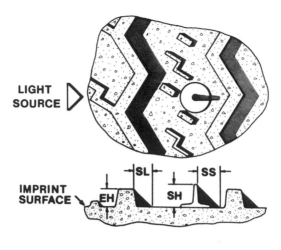

SS : Spike Shadow
SH : Spike Height
SL : Shadow Length          $EH = \dfrac{SH \times SL}{SS}$
EH : Element Height

**Figure 7.8.**   3-D golf ball spotter used in a tire imprint photograph.

tree height.) This same system will apply to estimating the depth of tread features in a plastic tire imprint. A circular golf ball spotter, with the spike sticking up, combines these two basic principles (see Figure 7.8). (Remember, all tire imprints should be enhanced with oblique lighting.)

### Using a 3-D Golf Ball Spotter Scale

Golf ball spotters are used to mark a go 'fer's ball when he or she gets on the green. This simple and generally available object can be easily placed on the tread surface plane and should be included among the investigator's or photographer's equipment. A golf ball spotter may be equally effective for scale when photographing bite marks, shoe prints, or a number of other imprints. When photographing tire imprints using a three-dimensional golf ball spotter scale, use the following procedure:

1. Place one golf ball spotter in an open area near the center of the imprint image spike sticking up.
2. Align the camera parallel to the tread surface plane (approximately 30 inches above imprint).

3. Use an oblique flash from one side of the imprint at approximately a 45-degree angle (take a second shot with the flash on the opposite side).
4. Retain the spotter for scale when developing 1 : 1 print, *or* clearly mark the spotter with the diameter of the circle and the spike height so that dimensions are visible in the photographic image.
5. If the end of the spike is ground flat and marked with a contrasting color (black or white), measurements will be more accurate. The ball spotter should also be of a tone that contrasts with the imprint surface.
6. Refer to Figure 7.8 for calculations:

Measure spike height (SH).

Measure spike shadow (SS).

Measure shadow length (SL) of questioned raised elements.

Use formula to calculate element height (EH).

*Note:* Because the flash is relatively close to the imprint, shadow measurements will be most accurate if they are taken within a few inches of the golf ball spotter (see Figure 7.9).

Recognizing the fact that nothing is new, that apparently new ideas are only adaptations of previously developed ideas, I want to give credit to those involved in the golf ball spotter scale idea:

1. The disk for horizontal scale was introduced to me by William Hyzer through his articles in *Photomethods Magazine* (1981 and 1986).

**Figure 7.9.** Typical tire imprint with golf ball spotter used for 3-D scale. (*Courtesy of W. G. Hyzer, forensic photogrammetry expert*)

2. Robert Yeager used a distortion-free dimensional vertical scale with oblique lighting to measure depths in 360-degree photographs of tire treads at Smithers Scientific Services in Akron, Ohio.
3. The additional idea of using a vertical projection to determine flash height and angle when reconstructing known tracks was suggested by Ernest Hamm.

## Connecting Photo Imprints

If a full revolution or a long section of a tire track is available, a sequence of connecting and overlapping exposures should be taken. It is important to have on the identification cards a series of numbers keyed to the exposures so that later the prints can be put in the correct order. Correlating pictures can be achieved by placing a long tape adjacent to the total impression, but this tape does not preclude the need for a scale at the same plane as the imprint.

## Taking the Photograph

Now the examiner can finally take the pictures. First, position the camera directly over the tire imprint with the film plane parallel to the imprint. I recommend *two* exposures for each sequence, one at normal exposure and one at two stops overexposed. The reason for a second exposure two stops overexposed is to achieve greater detail in the shadow areas. Take your time, and if in doubt take additional photographs. Remember, photographs of tire imprints may help positively establish a suspect's vehicle at the scene of the crime.

It is expected that the investigator will have a basic understanding of photography and be capable of operating modern photographic equipment, but he or she may wish to enlist the services of department specialists or civilian professionals. If professionals are used, it will be necessary to advise them of the procedures outlined here. I have not worked on a single case where the type of camera, the type of film used, or the absence of a tripod affected the outcome of the investigation. The photographic equipment is not as critical as the ability of the photographer to follow these basic rules:

1. Photograph all suspect tire imprints.
2. Include a scale.
3. Include an identification card.
4. Make the camera film plane parallel to the imprint.
5. Use oblique lighting.

## Enlargements

After the film is developed, review all exposures and the results of the oblique lighting. The best-quality photographs should be enlarged—one-to-one or full size.

*If there is no suspect,* enlargements will be used for a variety of identification procedures (see Chapter 10). *If there is a suspect,* enlargements will be used for preparing screen positives (see Chapter 14).

## Screen Positives

Screen positives are the most effective way of making a visual comparison between crime scene impressions and tire test impressions. They are made directly from the original full size continuous tone black and white print. Light areas are light, dark areas are dark. I recommend using 133 screen pattern or greater; because of the cost the examiner should study all prints for pertinent details before ordering screen positives of all imprints.

### Photographic Overlays: Definitions and Recommendations

*Transparencies* (a projected material, normally in color): 35 mm film, normally called "35 mm slide." The 4″ × 5″ or 8″ × 10″ sizes are usually called transparencies.

*"Kodalith":* This is a registered trademark of Eastman Kodak Co. The same as "graphic arts film" (below).

*Graphic arts "Kodalith" film* (high-contrast transparent material): A high-contrast material on a clear base that produces an image without gray areas. Any dark areas become black; any light areas become clear.

*Screen Kodalith* (half-tone): A screen pattern used for reproducing a continuous tone print for reproduction purposes. Screens available in 65, 85, 100, 110, 120, 133, 150, 175, and 200 lines per square inch.

*Screen negative:* The reverse of the original continuous tone print. Light areas become dark, dark areas become light.

*Screen positive:* The positive or the same as the original continuous tone print. Light areas are light, dark areas are dark.

I recommend using *screen positives,* 133 screen pattern or greater. Lithographers may charge approximately $30 for a 12″ × 18″ screen positive with 133 lines. Because of the cost, I recommend that the examiner should study all prints for pertinent details before requesting screen positives of all prints and, then finding that some are unnecessary.

## Recording Photographs

Even though much information is listed on the imprint identification card, an accurate record should be kept in the investigator's notebook. To aid in documenting the photographs, some agencies furnish official photo logs or forms for use at a crime scene. In some jurisdictions it may be necessary to document the chain of custody of those responsible for handling the film.

In his book *Practical Homicide Investigation* Vernon Geberth (1983) states that the following photo information should be recorded:

1. The date and time
2. The exact location
3. A brief description of the detail being photographed
4. The compass direction (North, South, East, or West)
5. The focus distance
6. The type of film and camera utilized
7. Any special equipment utilized
8. Light and weather conditions
9. The number of exposures
10. The identity of the photographer

Geberth continues:

The photographer should keep possession of the exposed film for delivery to the laboratory for processing. After these photos are developed, the above information should be entered either on the back of each photograph or on an appropriate form indicating each photo by number.

The comprehensive log is necessary to assure the admissibility of the crime scene photos in court. The log includes the ten points mentioned above, as well as the chain of custody from exposures to final disposition and storage of the film and negatives.

In addition, the police laboratory should keep an evidence log containing the following information:

1. The identity of the individual delivering the film for process (name, rank, serial number, etc.)
2. Date and time the film was received for processing
3. Results of development
4. Number of prints requested
5. Location of original negatives
6. Identity of the person receiving developed prints and/or negatives if there is no central storage

In the event that a commercial laboratory is used to process the film, the management should be requested to cooperate in adhering to the rules of evidence handling. This should include limiting the number of personnel handling the evidence film, as well as guaranteeing the security of the film and negatives. Needless to say, the commercial firm utilized to process any evidentiary material should be a reputable establishment.

In the case described below, the photographer made very good reproductions, but his records were poor.

### Case Study 7.1

Tire imprints were left in the sand at a homicide case. I was given photographs of individual tire imprints and test imprints from a suspect's vehicle. I made my comparisons and found that I could make a positive identification with many "specific accidental characteristics."

Unfortunately, however, the photographer had not labeled the individual photographs, and he did not make a scene sketch showing the location of each tire imprint. In addition, the general scene photo was not descriptive of the individual imprint locations, and the tire tracks were poorly recorded in the investigator's notebook. Two years after the homicide, a trial was held. By then the photographer had forgotten many significant details, and his records were too sketchy to be of much help.

My testimony followed his and was entirely contingent on the photographs I had received. The defense attorney discredited the photographer's testimony so completely that it weakened my testimony. For a variety of reasons, the suspect was not convicted.

## Photographic Equipment

The 4 × 5 format camera has the advantage of a large negative for enlargements, but the 35 mm single-lens reflex camera or the 120 mm medium-format camera is generally available and quite satisfactory. A tripod and cable release for either camera is advisable but not required. Black-and-white film is preferred, but if only color film is available, use that. The enlargements will then be made in black and white. Color is not important with tire imprints. Slow-speed film is recommended.

The following photographic material is the suggested minimum:

A 35 mm single-lens reflex camera or a 120 mm medium-format camera with a normal lens

A tripod

A shutter release cable, if there is no self-timer on the camera

An electronic flash

A 5-foot sync cord (flash to camera)

A low ASA black-and-white film (i.e., 25–100 ASA)

A scale

Identification cards

A large pen

## An Unidentified Tire Imprint Photo Collection: Suggested Administrative Procedure

This basic procedure was presented by Michael J. Cassidy for collection of footwear impressions (Cassidy 1980). This procedure might apply equally well to police identification sections that are aggressively recording tire imprints.

1. Each identification section will maintain a collection of unidentified crime scene tire imprints. The actual method for this system can be flexible, but it should be set up so that the items in the collection can be easily compared with tire imprints of known criminals and other unsolved cases involving tire imprint evidence.
2. Unidentified tire imprints should be kept in this collection at least six months, as local conditions, the size of the collection, and other factors determine.
3. Imprints are to be enlarged to one standard size, preferably 1 : 1.
4. All relevant data, such as tread width and wheelbase and tire tread stance measurements (if available), cross reference information regarding other files, and information on other tire designs or patterns filed for the same type of offense are to be recorded with these imprints.
5. Use the following tire imprint classification system in Figure 7.10, which is designed to make retrieval and association of tire imprints more effective and is to be adhered to as closely as possible. The majority of tread patterns consist of the types shown in Figure 7.10 and may be filed according to the categories in that figure.

## Conclusion

In my teaching at various police academies in the United States and Canada, crime scene investigators have told me that the potential value of tire imprint photographs has been greatly underestimated. General crime scene photographs often include photographs of tire tracks and a notation is made in the report about tire tracks, but then it is simply filed away.

**Rib**              **Aggressive Rib**      **Rib / Cross Bar**      **Cross Bar**

**Block**            **Directional**         **All Season**           **Curvilineal**

**Figure 7.10.** Types of tread patterns.


Using photography to record tire imprints is within the capability of the average investigator. Photography is an essential element of professional law enforcement. The investigator should photograph tire imprints as described above or preserve the scene until a more professional photographer arrives. *The balance of material described in the following chapters will be of little value if this basic photographic procedure is not followed.*

# Wheelbase and Tire Tread Stance Measurements 8

*The ultimate goal of the tire track investigation is the identification of the vehicle producing the track.*

(Given, Nehrich, Shields 1977)

The following information and service was graciously provided by the Michigan State Police East Lansing Forensic Laboratory.

The wheelbase and tire tread stance measurements taken at the scene of a crime may either be unique to a single manufacturer or model vehicle or be characteristic of a general class of vehicles. Also, some O.E. (original equipment) tires are supplied only to specific manufacturers or even specific models. The combination of vehicle dimensions and tire design identification can assist in identifying a single make and model vehicle.

It is important to note that wheelbase and tire tread stance measurements should be taken only *after* photography and/or casting is completed. Measurements are difficult to make without damaging a key portion of the tire imprint, so save measurement for last.

## Taking and Using the Measurements

The computer of the Scientific Laboratories Section of the Michigan State Police has the manufacturers' specifications for the wheelbases and front and rear tire tread stances for both American and foreign vehicles. This list includes measurements for passenger cars, pickup trucks, vans, and four-wheel-drive vehicles.

The investigator should try to obtain three measurements:

1. Wheelbase (distance from front axle to rear axle)
2. Front tire tread stance (distance from center to center of front tires)
3. Rear tire tread stance (distance from center to center of rear tires)

Only one of the above measurements is necessary for a computer search. But if two, or ideally all three, measurements are used, a more accurate and smaller number of possible matches may be obtained.

The front and rear stance measurements on most vehicles vary. For most American vehicles the rear tire tread stance is more narrow than the front tire tread stance.

Tire tread stance measurements should be made with accuracy to the nearest 1/8 inch and when the track is going in a straight line. Wheel alignment (camber, tow-in, etc.) will slightly alter tread stance dimensions from the original manufacturer's specification. Oversize tires usually will not vary from the original specification if the original rims are still on the vehicle.

The wheelbase dimensions can be difficult or impossible to obtain. If a vehicle traveled in a straight line, stopped, and then continued in a straight line, it may not be possible to observe measuring points.

Figure 8.1 illustrates one method of obtaining the wheelbase measurements of a vehicle that has changed its direction of travel by stopping then turning while backing. Measurements are taken from the leading edge of the front tire to the leading edge of the rear tire. As an example, if the three measurements in Figure 8.1 were found to be 103.0 inches for the wheelbase and 55.5 inches for the front and rear stance, a computer search would show a match for a 1970 Ford Maverick only. If all three measurements cannot be obtained, then a

**Figure 8.1.** One method for obtaining wheelbase measurements. (*Courtesy of Roger J. Bulhouse, Michigan State Police*)

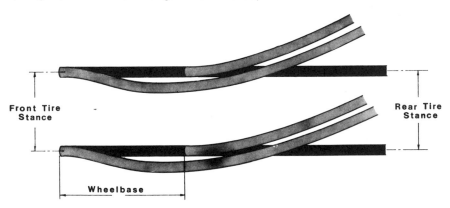

Front Tire
Stance

Rear Tire
Stance

Wheelbase

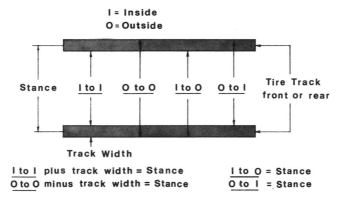

I = Inside
O = Outside

Stance | I to I | O to O | I to O | O to I | Tire Track front or rear

Track Width

I to I plus track width = Stance     I to O = Stance
O to O minus track width = Stance     O to I = Stance

**Figure 8.2.** Different methods of obtaining tire track stance. (*Courtesy of Roger J. Bulhouse, Michigan State Police*)

computer search will come up with an increased number of possible matches.

To be sure which are the front tracks and which are the rear tracks, the investigator must determine the direction of travel and what maneuvers the vehicle performed. When measuring the front and rear stances, measure the track in a number of different ways to ensure accuracy (see Figure 8.2).

The data entered into the computer can be varied plus or minus any amount, depending on how accurate the investigating officer feels the measurement is. Table 8.1 shows a typical printout sent to the investigating officer.

**Table 8.1.** Sample Typical Computer Printout in Computer Search

| TRUCK FILE SEARCH | | | | 82.08.02 AT 15.34 |
|---|---|---|---|---|
| Search parameters: | | | | |
| Wheelbase: Minimum 102.0 | | | | Maximum 103.0 |
| Front stance: Minimum 53.8 | | | | Maximum 54.2 |
| Rear stance: Minimum 52.0 | | | | Maximum 52.4 |

| W.B. | Front | Rear | Year | Make/Model |
|---|---|---|---|---|
| 102.4 | 54.0 | 52.2 | 1982 | Chevrolet/Luv Mini Pickup short bed |
| 102.4 | 54.0 | 52.2 | 1981 | Chevrolet/Luv Mini Pickup |
| 102.4 | 54.0 | 52.2 | 1980 | Chevrolet/Luv Mini Pickup |
| 102.4 | 54.0 | 52.2 | 1979 | Chevrolet/Luv Mini Pickup short bed |
| 102.4 | 54.0 | 52.2 | 1978 | Chevrolet/Luv Mini Pickup |
| 102.4 | 54.0 | 52.2 | 1977 | Chevrolet/Luv Mini Pickup |

*Source:* Courtesy of Roger J. Bulhouse, Michigan State Police.

## Identifying Vehicles from Turning Diameter

The Micro-Chemical Unit of the East Lansing Forensic Laboratory has the turning circle diameter measurements of many U.S. and foreign vehicles on file. This measurement can be used to help identify a vehicle used in the commission of a crime. The investigator must determine which is the outside front track and make measurements on this track at the point where it appears to be the tightest arc.

The turning diameter of a vehicle may be determined by taking two measurements at the scene (see Figure 8.3):

1. Determine the length of a cord (C) across the arc made by the outside front tire.
2. Measure the distance from the center of the cord to the nearest point on the arc (M).

The investigator may either use the formula for calculating the turning diameter or submit the two measurements to the East Lansing Forensic Laboratory to do the figuring and to search listings of vehicle measurements. The turning diameter measurement is most useful when the vehicle is turning with the wheel fully locked (Michigan State Police 1982). *I feel that turning diameter dimensions may only help eliminate some vehicles.* I have not had experience taking wheelbase and tire tread stance measurements at a crime scene, because I can only work with what is furnished. I understand that the computer printout provided by the East Lansing Forensic laboratory is very effective and continually updated. A noted forensic tire consultant in England, R. J. Grogan, finds these wheelbase and tire tread stance vehicle dimensions to be "a powerful weapon in his armoury."

**Figure 8.3.**   Measuring the turning diameter of a vehicle. Key:  C = chord; M = median. (*Courtesy of Roger J. Bulhouse, Michigan State Police*)

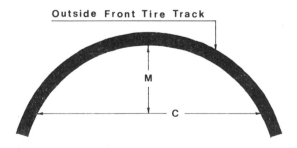

Outside Front Tire Track

M

C

Turning Diameter (T. D.)

$$\text{T.D.} = 2 \left( \frac{(C)^2}{8M} + \frac{M}{2} \right)$$

In addition, Dunlop Limited's tabulation of all vehicles sold in the United Kingdom is now computerized (Grogan 1978).

I have analyzed many tire imprints from various crime scenes and have observed that the right rear tire is more likely to make an imprint than the other tire positions. This may be (1) because rear tire tracks generally obliterate the front tire tracks when proceeding forward, or (2) because the right side of the vehicle more often gets off on the side of the road, where imprints are more visible.

# A Tire Imprint Identification System

**9**

*Science's fundamental advantage over common sense rests in a single word—System.*

(Huber 1959–60)

This chapter provides a logical system for analyzing tire impressions. Such attempts to establish a system are addressing the needs of examiners, expert witnesses, and the legal community. The "Tire Imprint Identification Checklist" (Table 9.1) can be used to help prepare a case or write a report, and examiners may find it to be valuable as a visual display when presenting evidence to a jury. The examiner should review each item listed for consistency with the evidence available, proceeding from left to right.

Tire characteristics can be divided into two basic headings: class and accidental. Class characteristics can be further divided into brand vs. brand and mold vs. mold as shown in Table 9.1.

## Brand vs. Brand (see Figure 9.1)

The imprint features of an unknown tire brand, preserved from the crime scene, are compared with the imprint features of a known tire brand. Each pertinent feature should be reviewed.

## Mold vs. Mold (see Figure 9.2)

The next consideration is to check for consistent mold features. It is possible to have consistent brand features but determine that the imprint was actually made from a mold different from the one that produced the suspect tire.

**Table 9.1.** Tire Imprint Identification Checklist

| | Class Characteristics | | | Accidental Characteristics | |
| --- | --- | --- | --- | --- | --- |
| **A.** Brand vs. Brand | | **B.** Mold vs. Mold | **C.** General | | **D.** Specific |
| 1 | Element shape | 1 Mold offset | 1 Circumferential wear | 1 Cuts |
| 2 | Number of ribs | 2 Tread wear indicators | 2 Lateral wear | 2 Tears |
| 3 | Groove shape | 3 Mold variations | 3 Cupping wear | 3 Chunk outs |
| 4 | Sipe pattern | 4 Serial side in | 4 Heel and toe wear | 4 Stone holding |
| 5 | Noise treatment | vs. | 5 Skid depth | 5 Texture variations |
| 6 | Arc width | Serial side out | 6 Exposed tie bars | 6 Abrasions |
| 7 | Notches | | 7 Furrow wear | 7 Side treatment variations |
| 8 | Slots | | 8 Feathering | |
| 9 | Percent void | | | |
| 10 | Stud pattern | | | |
| 11 | Side treatment | | | |
| 12 | Round shoulder | | | |
| | vs. | | | |
| | Square shoulder | | | |
| 13 | Black sidewalls | | | |
| | vs. | | | |
| | White sidewalls | | | |
| | vs. | | | |
| | Raised white letters | | | |

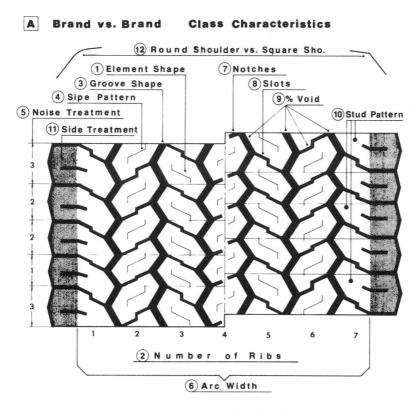

**Figure 9.1.** Typical tire brand features to be checked.

**Figure 9.2.** Typical tire features resulting from mold variations.

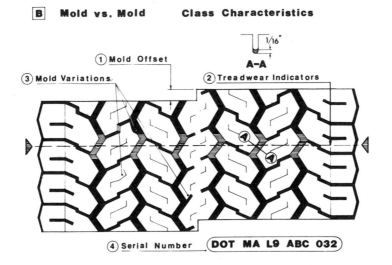

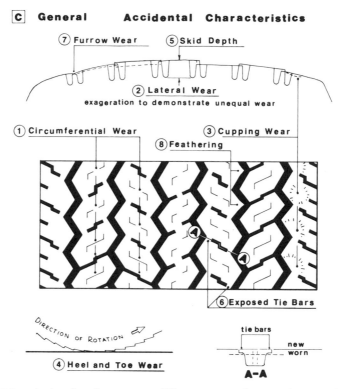

**Figure 9.3.** A tire develops many different general wear characteristics.

If all class characteristics are consistent, then proceed to accidental characteristics.

Accidental (happening by chance) characteristics can be divided into two basic headings: general and specific.

General accidental wear characteristics can be observed and a comparison of these features should be thorough (see Figure 9.3). If all pertinent features are consistent, then specific characteristics should be reviewed. If specific characteristics are identified, and all the previous categories are consistent, a positive identification can be made (see Figure 9.4).

There may be a temptation for some investigators to jump ahead looking for general and/or specific accidental characteristics. This should never be done; always check each pertinent item in each of the categories.

Because it is important to understand each checklist feature, a glossary of terms and the figures showing graphically displayed tread features should be thoroughly understood.

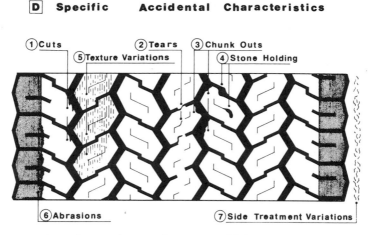

**Figure 9.4.**  Specific tire damage features and locations are unique.

## Class Characteristics

Investigators should examine all tread pattern features common to one specific tire design or brand of tire.

### A. Brand vs. Brand

The following terms, explanations, and schematics as shown in Figure 9.1 describe the significant features to be reviewed. It is important that all tread design items listed are consistent before proceeding further with the checklist.

1. *Element shape:* The rubber portion of the tread, bound by grooves and/or slots. Provides wearing surface and road contact that enable the driver to steer and stop.
2. *Number of ribs:* The rubber elements of the tire tread that come in contact with the ground, oriented in a generally circumferential direction (the schematic tread shown in Figure 9.2 has seven ribs). Not all treads have definable ribs.
3. *Groove shape:* Large void areas adjacent to ribs or elements. Grooves permit an easy, fast escape for water and give the tread edges a direct, positive grip on the surface being traveled.
4. *Sipe pattern:* Narrow slots molded into the ribs of the tread design to improve the traction ability of the tire on wet pavement.
5. *Noise treatment:* A method of varying the size of the tread elements in a specific sequence to reduce tire noise.
6. *(Tread) "arc" width:* The lateral distance between the outer edges of the tire tread, measured on the tread surface.

7. *Notches:* A closed indentation off a major groove to improve traction.
8. *Slots:* Narrow grooves connecting major grooves to improve traction.
9. *Percent void:* The ratio of the groove and slot area relative to the total tread area.
10. *Stud pattern:* A varied arrangement of holes to accommodate studs for maximum winter effectiveness, found in some snow tires. Generally located in the outer shoulder ribs, or lugs, where there is a concentration of load.
11. *Side treatment:* The information and features occurring from the tread edge to the bead.
12. *Round shoulder vs. square shoulder:* The outer edges of the tire tread connecting with the sidewall may be molded round or square. Tires also wear round or square due to position, inflation, or handling.
13. *Black sidewalls vs. white sidewalls vs. raised white letters:* Black sidewalls will make a different impression against a wall or in deep soft impressions than white sidewalls or raised white letters will.

## B. Mold vs. Mold

The following terms, explanations and schematics as shown in Figure 9.2 describe the significant features to be reviewed. Mold variation may not exist or be apparent, but should be reviewed.

1. *Mold offset:* Sometimes referred to as mold rotation. Most tire molds have two halves, parting on a center rib. One half can be rotated or offset from the other half. Offsets may be intentional or nonintentional. Generally this is a small deviation from the tread drawing.
2. *Tread wear indicators:* Sometimes referred to as "wear bars." When the tread is worn down to one-sixteenth of an inch, narrow strips of smooth rubber will appear across the tread. Generally, six or more tread wear indicators are equally spaced around the tire circumference. Some brands have an arrow on the upper sidewall to help locate the indicators. The circumferential orientation of tread wear indicators to the tread sequence of pitches may vary from one mold to another.
3. *Mold variations:* Damaged molds can produce many tires before being corrected or replaced. One of the most common variations is bent sipes.
4. *Serial side in vs. serial side out:* Not all white sidewall tires are mounted with the white side *out.* Not all black sidewall tires are

mounted with the serial side *in*. Appearance is generally the motive for variation.

## Accidental Characteristics

Investigators should examine all tire wear and damage features resulting from both general and specific accidental conditions.

### C. General

The following terms, explanations, and schematics as shown in Figure 9.3 describe the significant features to be reviewed. Tires develop many different wear characteristics. Tire inflation, miles driven, road surface, tire/wheel balance, mechanical irregularities, driving habits, and tread design are a few of the many normal factors influencing general wear characteristics.

1. *Circumferential wear:* An unbalanced tire and wheel assembly may create irregular tread wear around the tire periphery.
2. *Lateral wear:* Misalignment in the front or rear, improperly operating brakes or shock absorbers, bent wheels, sprung axle housings, worn bushings, and so on, can cause uneven tread wear.
3. *Cupping wear:* Slight depressions can occur, primarily in the outer ribs, at regularly or irregularly spaced intervals. Sometimes this is more apparent in a test impression than when looking directly at the tire. This may be the result of out-of-balance wheels or worn shock absorbers or ball joints.
4. *Heel and toe wear:* Some designs, particularly lateral bar or aggressive all-season designs, are more subject to wearing on the leading edge of the tread element. The trailing edge will then stick up, forming a saw-toothed wear pattern.
5. *Skid depth (nonskid):* The remaining distance from tread surface to groove base.
6. *Exposed tie bars:* As tires wear, their appearance may change. Sipes generally show the greatest change with wear. If a section of a sipe or groove wears out before the remaining portion of a sipe or groove, that section is called a tie bar. The tie bars help stabilize the tread elements, reducing squirm in the footprint.
7. *Furrow wear:* This circumferential trench-type wear is seen primarily on heavy-duty rib truck tires. The points of the zigzag grooves are less supported, scrub more, and therefore wear more rapidly.
8. *Feathering:* The condition is the development of feather edges on the ribs, almost always due to incorrect toe.

*D. Specific*

The following terms, explanations, and schematics as shown in Figure 9.4 describe the significant features to look for. These are unique damage features in an exact location of a tire.

1. *Cuts:* Gashes from sharp foreign objects can occur anywhere on the tread. Generally they are most severe along the leading edges of tread elements.
2. *Tears:* Tears occur when tread elements pull apart or separate by force. This is most common at the apex of major grooves or sipes, where there is a flexing action.
3. *Chunk outs:* Excessive movement of tread elements or hardening with age can cause rubber to be torn off by rough road surfaces.
4. *Stone holding:* Foreign objects can become lodged in any size groove or sipe. Stones may be retained for thousands of miles, producing a bulge in that area. This is the most common specific characteristic to be observed.
5. *Texture variations:* The normally smooth tread surface may vary due to the interaction with the road surface, developing striations, indentations, or scoring along the direction of travel.
6. *Abrasions:* Wearing away of rubber shreds by friction, most commonly resulting from high-speed and locked-wheel braking, producing patches of abrasion in the tread surface. These abrasion patterns are always at right angles to the direction of travel. Abrasion may also occur on the shoulder and sidewall.
7. *Side treatment variations:* As with the tread surface, the sidewall may be damaged in many ways. Tire sidewalls can develop fatigue cracks, also referred to as weather checks.

As investigators become more experienced, the list of characteristics will undoubtedly expand. For instance, if a tire collected and retained a substance unique to the crime scene, this would be a "general accidental characteristic" that should be examined. If a tire repair is discovered, this would be a good "specific accidental characteristic." Also, when a larger diameter or wider tire than specified is used on a vehicle, it is possible for the tire to abrade or score on some part of the vehicle's body, steering, or suspension system. In addition, special application tires may have features unique to their function. The Tire Imprint Identification Checklist is in no way meant to be limiting.

# What Can Be Learned Without a Suspect's Vehicle

# 10

This chapter outlines the procedure for identifying tire imprints if you *do not* have a suspect's vehicle. The five case studies at the end of the chapter provide concrete examples of tire imprint identification procedures under such circumstances. Chapter 14 covers the procedure for identification when the suspect's vehicle *is* available.

After tire imprints have been recorded, begin the tire imprint identification procedure outlined in Figure 10.1.

## Prepare Photo Enlargements

Photo enlargements of the tire imprints should be prepared to actual size or 1 : 1.

## Identify All Imprints

If multiple tire imprints are discovered, identify all imprints thoroughly (see Figure 10.2). Even if imprints of apparently the same design

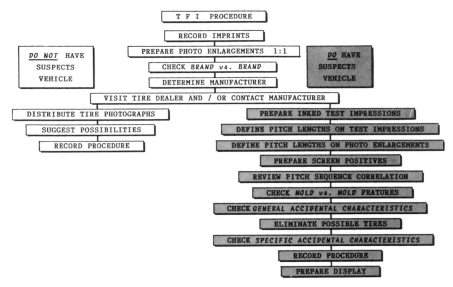

**Figure 10.1.** Tire imprint identification procedure when suspect's tire is not available.

**Figure 10.2.** Multiple tire imprints. (*Courtesy of Robert J. Link, Attorney and Counselor-at-Law*)

are discovered or are of poor quality, they should all be recorded. Different designs, tire sizes, or various general wear characteristics on the same vehicle will significantly increase the probability of making an identification.

## Determine Shoulder Rib or Outer Edge of Imprint

Determine the shoulder rib or outer edge of the imprint. Radial tire shoulder ribs generally have transverse slots. Most new passenger tires have round shoulders and wear wider and rounder, particularly in the front position. This makes it difficult to measure an exact edge to the shoulder rib. Next determine the center rib. Most tires have a rib in the center of the tire that is often more narrow than the neighboring ribs, looks different, and has fewer cross slots. Tire molds generally part on the center rib, so a blank circumferential line may appear in the center of the center rib. Because most tires are symmetrical, it is not essential to have the full width tire imprint to establish design and size.

## Determine the Tread Pattern

Determine the basic category of the tread pattern—for instance, not all tires have circumferential ribs. Tread designs vary for different purposes—high speed, wet traction, snow traction, durability, or combinations for all-season use. In the future, new categories of tread designs will evolve. Basic tread patterns may be grouped as in Figure 7.10.

## Become Acquainted with the *Tread Design Guide*

The *Tread Design Guide* can help determine the tire design name and brand. The *Who Makes It? and Where? Directory* should also be used to help identify the manufacturer or distributor. The *Tread Design Guide* is the only good source of tread designs compiled into one book. It is published yearly and contains photographs of each tire and information about the following:

Passenger tires

Highway-type truck tires

Off-the-road tires

Agricultural tires

Motorcycle tires

Passenger and truck retread tires

Standard and custom wheels

Because a suspect's tire may have been discontinued, *Tread Design Guides* going back a number of years should be reviewed. These books are a must for tire tread examiners, who should always have the latest one. (See the end of Chapter 3 for how to order.)

## Determine Which Year of the *Tread Design Guide* to Use

Because the *Tread Design Guide* is updated annually, determine which years to check. As a guideline, radial tires are more current, and bias and bias-belted tires are older. In determining tire construction, it is helpful to understand the cycle patterns shown in Chapter 1, Figures 1.6, 1.7, 1.8, and 1.9. For example, a bias tire imprint will generally have more contracted grooves than a radial tire imprint. The more-open tread patterns, such as the all-season passenger or truck designs, are generally more current radial tires. Try bracketing the guides in three-year increments to simplify the search. Examiners may find it necessary to look through three or more books for a complete listing. A private-brand design may be sold to new distributors yearly and deleted from others periodically. Typically, designs will stay in existence for more than five years; tire molds are expensive to scrap.

## Determine What Type of Vehicle Made the Imprint

Determine whether the imprint was made by a passenger or truck or other type of tire. This often requires experience. Generally, larger tread widths are on trucks because larger tire sizes are needed to carry the greater loads. Exceptions are high-performance passenger tires. Another confusion is that passenger tires are often used on small pickup trucks. If in doubt, check all the passenger, truck, and retread sections.

## Trace Over Main Distinguishable Features in Crime Scene

Using very transparent tracing paper, trace over the main distinguishable features in the crime scene impression. Fix the basic shapes in your mind before looking in the *Tread Design Guide*. Do not try to look for more than one design at a time. Now scan the pages, looking for basic features, then list each possibility. Later, review the list and eliminate inconsistent designs with attention to further detail (see Case Study 10.2 in this chapter). Remember, groove and sipe features change from the new tire appearance shown in the *Guide* as tires wear (Figure 10.3). Sipes may be the last tread feature to check, because sipe appearance generally changes the most, due to wear.

**Figure 10.3.** Typical tire showing groove and sipe wear.

## Check "Brand vs. Brand"

Check "brand vs. brand" to see if a design that matches exactly can be identified, but *don't stop there.* If it appears to be a design for a private brand distributor, look further. The manufacturer may supply the same tread design to many distributors, and each distributor may have a different name on the tire sidewall (see Case Study 10.4 in this chapter).

## Determine the Manufacturer

Refer to the *Who Makes It? and Where? Directory* to determine the manufacturer. Brand names are cross-referenced with manufacturers or distributors. Check with a local dealer and/or contact the manufacturer.

## Visit the Tire Dealer

If there is a local dealer for the identified tire, visit the tire dealer to confirm your findings. The exact tire size should now be determined. Inked imprints could be made to confirm the size, but just a dirty tire driven over a light-colored cardboard may provide satisfactory confirmation. There is also a product specifically designed for recording tire imprints. "Acutread Tire Print Out" is a clean, rapid, and accurate method of recording tire impressions. A sample package of twenty 9" × 17" sheets costs approximately $35 plus freight. It may be purchased from Acutred Division of Notecare Inc., 2435 Professional Drive, Santa Rosa, CA 95403. The tire dealer may also know the types of vehicles that normally use a particular size tire (see Case Study 10.3 in this chapter).

## Contact the Manufacturer

Use the toll-free numbers listed in the *Who Makes It? and Where? Directory* and the *Consumer's Resource Handbook* to contact the manufacturer. Call the manufacturers' legal department, describe the case, and ask for any help they can give. Generally, the legal department can be of assistance and will also give clearance for you to be assisted by the development department. An engineer from the development department may have a broader understanding of tire usage than a tire dealer. The engineer handling the specific tire in question might know if the design is primarily sold to O.E. accounts, trade sales, or both (see Case Study 10.1 in this chapter). Ask for an 8″ × 10″ photograph of the tire to distribute to all investigators on the case. A three-quarters view, showing both tread and sidewall, is generally available (see Case Study 10.5 in this chapter).

## Contact the Manufacturer's Sales Department

Speak with someone in the manufacturer's sales department who is knowledgeable about the line of tires being examined. The number of sales can give an idea of distribution, O.E. sales vs. replacement sales, yearly production by size, sidewall features, and so on (see Chapter 3).

## Narrow Down the List of Possible Vehicles

It may now be possible to come up with possible vehicles that normally use this size tire (see Case Studies 10.1 and 10.3, in this chapter).

## Record Your Procedure

Record your identification procedure now, while it is still fresh in your mind. Your records will be useful if a suspect's vehicle becomes available, and they can help refresh your memory for conferring with another person or for testimony in court. In addition, the mere act of recording the procedure can help sharpen your awareness of the facts available. Francis Bacon put it best: "Reading maketh a full man, conference a ready man, and writing an exact man."

## Taking Tire Circumference Measurements

A long, even intermittent, tire imprint found at the scene of a crime will help establish tire size. After recording the imprint, look for a unique specific accidental characteristic that is repeated further along on the imprint. Measuring the distance between these repeated characteristics will give the rolling tire circumference.

If the tire design is established, the examiner should then contact a local dealer or the manufacturer. With a rolling tire circumference measurement that you provide, the tire manufacturer can convert that to tire rolling radii to help determine size. The combination of tire circumference and tread-width dimensions should give a fairly accurate indication of tire size. It may be necessary to take into account a worn tire that has a smaller outside diameter and be aware that some distortion may result in contracted lengths. Tire size can generally be determined only when the tread width is available. I have never had a long tire imprint given to me, but it is good to know that all this information is available.

### Case Study 10.1

Much information can be gleaned from a single photograph of questionable quality. In this case the photograph furnished (Figure 10.4) did not have a scale, but an identification tag did help develop a 1:1 enlargement. The imprint was good enough to determine that the tire imprint may have been made by a Toyo Z-709 design, which at the time was used primarily on 1980 Toyotas. Two models, the Cressida and the Celica, used this size P185/70SR14 tire.

**Figure 10.4.** Photograph of questionable quality. (*Courtesy of Hans P. Dara, Suffolk County [NY] Police Dept.* )

*Case Study 10.2*

This case shows the importance of the deduction process and of observing details, such as stud holes, in determining the likely tire position with a directional design.

In 1980 the Vero Beach, Florida, detective division was investigating a number of burglaries in which tire tracks were at the scene of the crimes. Very little other evidence was obtainable. I was sent a photograph, Figure 10.5, and asked to investigate. I was able to determine the following:

1. In the 1980 *Tread Design Guide* there is a similar design shown as an Alray "Ground Hawg" *without* stud holes and with raised white letters. Examining the imprint photograph closely, however, I observed that stud holes were visible even in the coarse sand (arrows highlight a few stud hole positions—see Figure 10.6) and could therefore conclude that this imprint was *not* made by an Alray "Ground Hawg" tire. But the 1980 *Tread Design Guide* also shows a similar Denman "Ground Hawg" design *with* stud holes (Figure 10.7).
2. The imprint was made by a Denman tire worn to the approximate depth of the shallow tie bars. This nearly eliminated most

**Figure 10.5.** Tire imprint from Vero Beach crime scene. (*Courtesy of Tom McAllister, Vero Beach* [FL] *Police Dept.*)

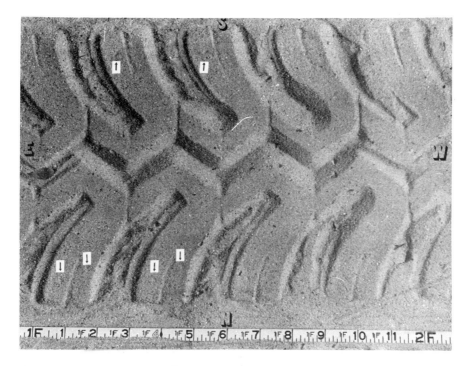

**Figure 10.6.** Tire imprint from Vero Beach crime scene; arrows show some stud holes that made identification possible.

**Figure 10.7.** Denman "Ground Hawg" tire with stud holes. (*Courtesy of Firestone Tire & Rubber Co.*)

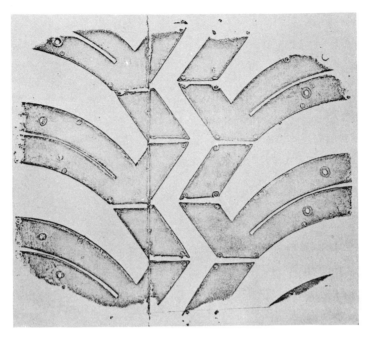

**Figure 10.8.** Inked tire print from Denman "Ground Hawg." (*Courtesy of Firestone Tire & Rubber Co.*)

of the center lateral slots that protrude from the apex of the lateral shoulder pockets.

3. The North side of the impression (N) (see Figure 10.6) is the more narrow side of the mold. This off-center parting is shown in the interruption of the transverse slot on the N side only.

4. The tread is directional (shoulder pockets all point in one direction). The narrow side of the mold is the back side of the tire. If the tire was properly mounted, one could assume that the imprint was made from a tire on the left side of the vehicle—probably the left rear, if moving forward. Almost all vehicles using tires like this at that time were rear-wheel drive, and because the rear tire imprint generally obliterates the front, I made this assumption.

5. The inked tire print (Figure 10.8) was made from a Denman "Ground Hawg" and illustrates mold offset at the parting line. The crime scene imprint also has a slight mold offset in the opposite direction. If a suspect with this tire design on the vehicle is apprehended, this "mold vs. mold" feature should be observed.

6. The Denman "Ground Hawg" is produced only with a black sidewall.
7. The tire imprint width suggests a 10–16.5 or 10–15 size.
8. This size tire is generally used on pickup trucks and RVs.
9. Denman Rubber Company in Warren, Ohio, could be consulted concerning distribution or stores in the Vero Beach area. Since this is a replacement tire, a tire registration check should be considered.

### Case Study 10.3

This case demonstrates that identifying a tire as original equipment can lead the investigator to specific model vehicles.

In November 1983 the Pensacola (Florida) Crime Laboratory Bureau asked me to "identify the tire manufacturer and any other data which may aid in the investigation." I received photographs of tire castings (Figure 10.9 and Figure 10.10) taken at the scene of a homicide. I was also told that the lab had studied five years of the *Tread Design Guide* without any luck.

A portion of my report stated: "I am positive the imprint was made by a Goodyear vector tire. A P175/80R13 size, overlay attached, fits rather well. This is only sold to Chrysler for their new 1984 vehicles. Some of those vehicles might be: Aries, Reliant, LeBaron, New Yorker E class, and Dodge 600." It is not surprising that the lab did not find the design. It was too new to be listed in the latest *Tread Design Guide.* I had the advantage of having previously studied the very same design and knowing that it was used by Chrysler at the time. It was the first curvilineal design I was aware of, and therefore very recognizable.

To confirm the design, size, and vehicle usage, I went to the nearest Chrysler dealer. After finding the tread width that matched, I ran the fully loaded dusty tire over a piece of clean white cardboard. The imprint was good and confirmed the design and size. The dealer was able to tell me exactly which vehicles used this size tire.

I later learned that the tire identification helped lead to the apprehension of the murderer. P175/80R13 Vector tires were found on his rented 1984 Reliant station wagon with only about 300 miles wear. The suspect confessed.

### Case Study 10.4

This case shows how important it is to review tread design guidebooks for *all* possible design names used for a particular tread design and to act promptly. The case involved multiple homicides.

**Figure 10.9.** Photograph of Goodyear Vector tire impression. (*Courtesy of Ottis W. Garrett, Florida Dept. of Law Enforcement*)

Good castings of a suspect's tires were available, and four photographs of tire castings were furnished: Figure 10.11, Figure 10.12, Figure 10.13, Figure 10.14.

The following is basically taken from my report:

I have examined RR casts 2, 3, 4, and 7 and find them to be a Firestone tire designated PBP253B-1. I am enclosing copies of a three-quarter view

**Figure 10.10.** Photograph of Goodyear Vector tire impression. (*Courtesy of Ottis W. Garrett, Florida Dept. of Law Enforcement*)

**Figure 10.11.** Tire casting 2 from multiple homicide case. (*Photograph furnished anonymously*)

**Figure 10.12.** Tire casting 3 from multiple homicide case. (*Photograph furnished anonymously*)

**Figure 10.13.** Tire casting 4 from multiple homicide case. (*Photograph furnished anonymously*)

**Figure 10.14.** Tire casting 7 from multiple homicide case. (*Photograph furnished anonymously*)

**Figure 10.15.** Three-quarter view of Firestone tire PBP253B-1 showing tread pattern. (*Courtesy of Firestone Tire & Rubber Co.*)

photograph showing the tread pattern (Figure 10.15). Also enclosed are copies of pages from the 1978 and 1981 *Tread Design Guide,* highlighting the design names these tires might have been sold under. The Firestone Tire & Rubber Company designed and manufactured all the following PBP253B-1 tread patterns.

*Identification for Casting Marked 2 LF*

*Source: Tread Design Guide, 1981,* p. 26 (Figure 10.16). *Note:* Picture in *Tread Design Guide* is reversed.
*Brand:* Cordovan
*Design:* Criterion steel-belted radial
*Distributed by:* Tire & Battery Corp., 4770 Hickory Hill Rd., Memphis, TN 38138

*Identification for Casting Marked 3*

*Source: Tread Design Guide,* 1981, p. 37 (Figure 10.17)
*Brand:* Falcon
*Design:* Falcon II steel-belted radial
*Distributed by:* Firestone-Fidesta Co.

*Identification for Casting Marked 4*

*Source: Tread Design Guide,* 1981, p. 57 (Figure 10.18). *Note:* Picture in *Tread Design Guide* is reversed.
*Brand:* Multi-Mile
*Design:* Criterion steel-belted radial

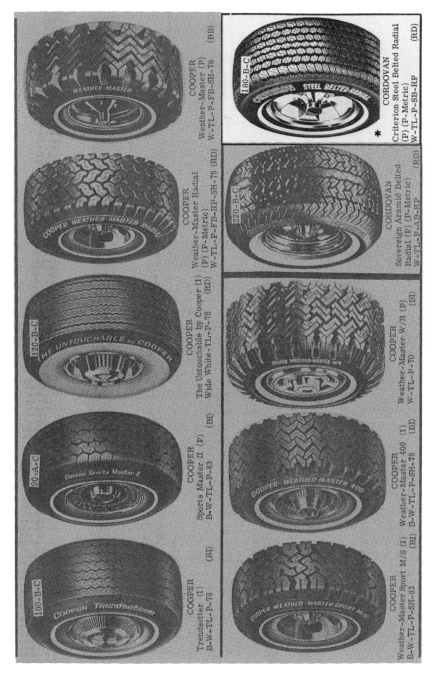

**Figure 10.16.** Criterion steel-belted radial. (*Courtesy of Al Snyder, editor, Tire Guides Inc.*)

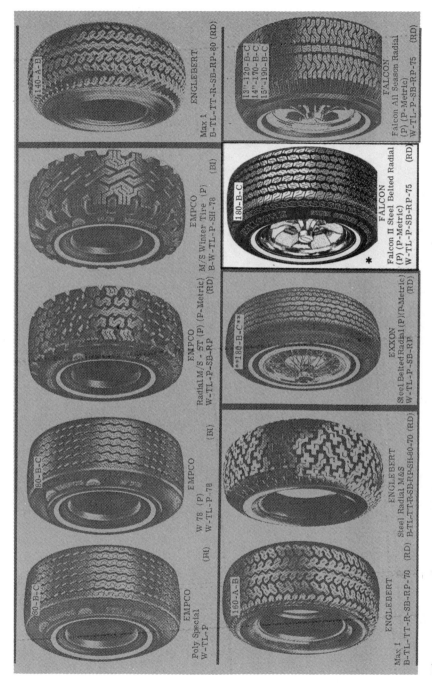

**Figure 10.17.** Falcon II steel-belted radial. (*Courtesy of Al Snyder, editor, Tire Guides Inc.*)

98

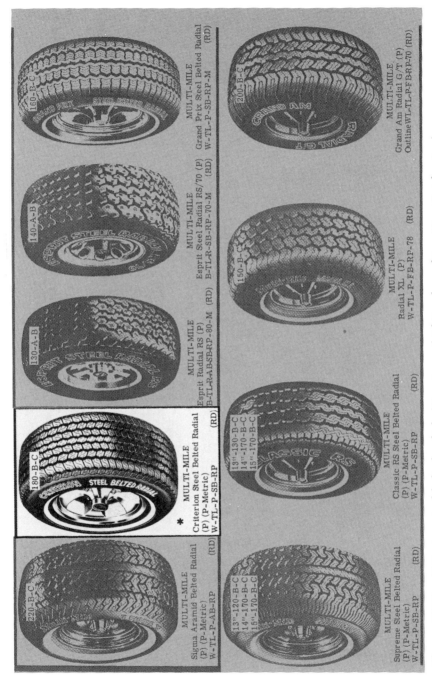

**Figure 10.18.** Criterion steel-belted radial. (*Courtesy of Al Snyder, editor, Tire Guides Inc.*)

*Distributed by:* Tire & Battery Corp., 4770 Hickory Hill Rd., Memphis, TN 38138

*Identification for Casting Marked 7*

*Source: Tread Design Guide,* 1978, p. 87 (Figure 10.19). *Note:* Picture in *Tread Design Guide* is reversed.

*Brand:* Union 76

*Design:* Steel-belted radial

*Distributed by:* Union Oil Company of California, 1650 East Golf Rd., Schaumberg, IL 60196

*Identification for Casting Marked 2 LR*

*Source: Tread Design Guide,* 1981, p. 48 (Figure 10.20).

*Brand:* Javelin

*Design:* Steel-belted radial

*Manufactured by:* Kelly Springfield

*Distributed by:* Zayre Corporation, 235 Old Conn. Path, Framingham, MA 01701

I have tread drawings of the seven-rib design shown in castings 2, 3, 4, and 7 that would be useful at a later date if a comparison is made with a suspect's tire imprint. Smaller sizes have a similar design in five-ribs. [It has already been noted that some manufacturers produce a five-rib design in small sizes and the same basic design in seven ribs for larger sizes. Unfortunately, only one size appears in the *Tread Design Guide.* In addition, tires are occasionally inadvertently shown in reverse image. That was true with the Cordovan, Union, and Multi-Mile photographs.]

I have examined the photograph of cast 2 and find that the left front imprint is of poor quality and very worn, but it appears to be a PBP253B-1 of a smaller size. The left rear imprint is similar in size and is a Javelin design, shown on page 48 of the 1981 *Tread Design Guide* enclosed. Cast imprints 3, 4, and 7 were apparently made by tires from a different vehicle than the cast imprint 2.

I find it interesting that the owner of the vehicle with smaller tires, shown in cast 2, also purchased the left front tire with the same tread pattern. This replacement-type tire is not very common, compared with original equipment tires. A tire registration check with emphasis on dealers in the state or region where the murder occurred could be undertaken.

The photographs you sent are of good quality, and the castings show much detail. If a suspect's tire(s) are found, they should be examined for accidental characteristics. [Unfortunately, the information I had was furnished to me more than one year after the castings were obtained. If the crime scene investigator had taken photographs of the total imprints, it would have been more beneficial than just the short castings. In addition, I was given no general scene photograph or sketch to help locate each imprint.]

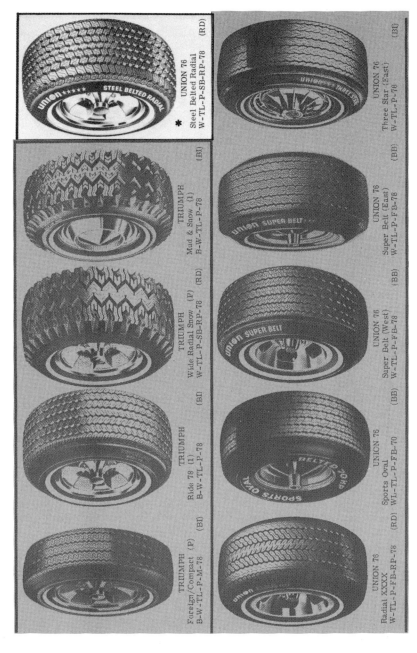

**Figure 10.19.** Steel-belted radial. (*Courtesy of Al Snyder, editor, Tire Guides Inc.*)

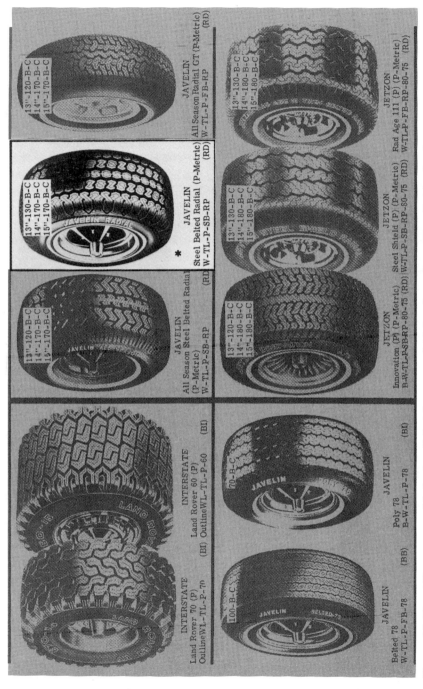

**Figure 10.20.** All-season steel-belted radial. (*Courtesy of Al Snyder, editor, Tire Guides Inc.*)

*Case Study 10.5*

To help illustrate the large amount of information that can be gained from a single tire track, I describe my first involvement with tire imprint identification. The 1976 case that launched me into this new career was a dual homicide in Monterey, California.

Two nude bodies of known prostitutes were found below a sand dune precipice. Many different tire tracks were found above the location. The investigating police observed that one pair of tire tracks had apparently been made by the vehicle transporting the women to that location. The driver's tennis shoe imprints were found to lead from the driver's side of the vehicle to the rear of the vehicle. The tracks then showed that the body of one woman was dragged across the rear tire track, then dropped over the embankment. The shoe imprints then proceeded to the front passenger side, where the driver apparently removed the second woman, dragging her heels in front of the vehicle. Then, returning to the vehicle, the suspect drove over the drag line and left the scene. This overlay of tracks fixed those specific tire imprints out of the many others in the area, as belonging to the vehicle that transported the women to the scene. Tire imprints were the only clues to the suspected murderer.

The police took pictures of the sandy tire imprint and circulated them to many local tire dealers, asking for identification of the tire design and the type of vehicle that would use this tire. Unfortunately, they received about as many suggestions as the number of dealers they contacted. One officer took the pictures to a nearby Firestone manufacturing plant, which was of no immediate help but sent the photographs to the home office in Akron, Ohio. One of my co-workers left the photographs on my desk with this note: "You won't be able to recognize this, will you?" I might not have pursued this new career if it had not been for that challenging note. "Somebody said it couldn't be done" says Edgar Guest's poem—and that's how I feel when challenged.

Unfortunately, the photograph (Figure 10.21) did not include the full tread width. First I determined the edge of the narrow shoulder rib, then I counted ribs and could see at least eight ribs. Tires generally have an odd number of ribs (the center rib is used to part the top half of the mold from the bottom half, so I expected nine or more ribs. Also, the fifth rib appeared to be different from the neighboring ribs in configuration. Assuming the fifth rib to be a center rib, I defined the tread design as having nine ribs.

My years of experience designing tires at Firestone led me to look first at the possibility that this was a Firestone tire. Firestone manufactured two lines of tires with nine ribs, and nine ribs were

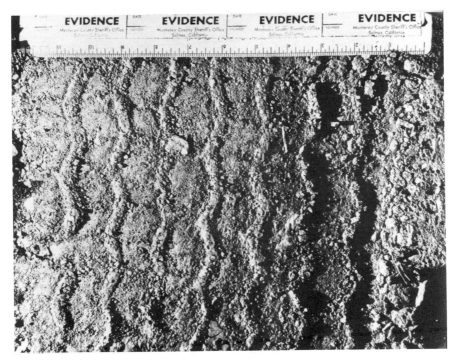

**Figure 10.21.** Photograph of sandy tire imprint in Monterey case. (*Courtesy of Investigative Staff Sgt. Terry Kaiser, Monterey County Sheriff's Dept., Salinas, Calif.*)

used only in the larger sizes of both designs. I quickly eliminated one of the designs, and focused my attention to the possibility that this was a large-size N50-15 Parnelli Jones design. All other small tires in the line had seven ribs (Figure 10.22).

I asked a draftsman to take the original tread drawings of the Parnelli Jones tire, and make an accurate drawing of one groove pitch sequence on tracing paper. This was used to overlay the correct groove in the photograph. The pattern and pitch lengths fit like a glove. My next step was to find a Parnelli Jones tire of the N50-15 size and make an overlay of the tread pattern with all its varying pitch lengths. It was again a thrill to find a beautiful fit.

I called the officer in the Monterey Police Department, explained who I was, and told him I had their tire imprint photographs and information that might be useful:

1. The tire imprint was made by an N50-15 Parnelli Jones design.

2. All Parnelli Jones tires are produced with raised white letters,

**Figure 10.22.** A seven-rib Parnelli Jones tire. (*Courtesy of Firestone Tire & Rubber Co.*)

which should make such a tire easy to notice on a stationary vehicle (see Figure 10.23).

3. The majority of these tires sold in California were at that time distributed through 13 different Parnelli Jones stores.

4. Most replacement tires are registered. The tire serial number and the purchaser's name and address are recorded. Firestone would agree, if so requested, to have a registration check made of all N50-15 Parnelli Jones tires sold in California.

**Figure 10.23.** Parnelli Jones tire with raised white letters. (*Courtesy of Firestone Tire & Rubber Co.*)

5. This size and design of tire would likely be on a high-performance or dune-buggy-type vehicle.

The Monterey police officer was amazed because they still had no clues, two weeks after the crime had been committed.

Two weeks later, in San Francisco, alert police arrested a man for molesting a prostitute. They had read in the newspaper about the Monterey homicides and called the Monterey police to see if there might be a connection. They were told that an Akron, Ohio tire designer said the suspect's tire imprints were made by N50-15 Parnelli Jones tires, probably on a high-performance vehicle, so they checked the suspect's car—it was a Camaro with four N50-15 Parnelli Jones tires!

The police later checked the suspect's apartment and found tennis shoes that looked similar to the footwear imprints found at the Monterey crime scene. The tire registration check showed the suspect's name on the list of purchasers. He confessed to both murders in Monterey.

This case was exciting, and ideal for an experienced tread designer. Admittedly, it was easier for me to recognize the tire because it was a Firestone tire I had worked on, and I had been involved with calculating the progressive noise treatment, which was an additional clue. It helps to be lucky on the first case—it builds confidence.

### Case Study 10.6

This case stresses the importance of prompt action in circulating photographs of the suspect's tire.

In 1981 a woman was abducted from a Lawson's store in Mansfield, Ohio, and raped and murdered. Her body was found the following day. Three days later an officer from the Mansfield police crime lab visited my office for tire identification assistance. He had photographs of plaster casts taken from tire impressions found next to the woman's body in a ditch along the side of a park road. A muddy imprint on the road was also photographed (see Figure 10.24).

That evening I was able to identify the rear tire impressions from the *Tread Design Guide* and the casting shown in Figure 10.25. They had been made by a small-size Ward's Traction Grip tire—one that, coincidentally, I had designed 10 years earlier (see Figure 10.26). Copies of that 8″ × 10″ tire photograph were supplied to the Mansfield patrolmen and detectives.

The next day I identified the front-tire castings as belonging to Jetzon Gemini IIs, manufactured by General (Figure 10.27). Be-

**Figure 10.24.** Photograph of muddy tire imprint in Mansfield, Ohio, case. (*Courtesy of M. M. Benick, Chief of Police, Mansfield, Ohio*)

**Figure 10.25.** Casting of Ward's Traction Grip tire imprint. (*Courtesy of Firestone Tire & Rubber Co.*)

**Figure 10.26.** Ward's Traction Grip tire. (*Courtesy of Firestone Tire & Rubber Co.*)

**Figure 10.27.** Casting of Jetzon Gemini II. (*Courtesy of M. M. Benick, Chief of Police, Mansfield, Ohio*)

**Figure 10.28.** Test impressions of suspect's vehicle tires in Mansfield, Ohio, case. (*Reprinted by permission of* Time *magazine*)

cause both front and rear tire treads were narrow, I suggested that the police look for a small vehicle with snow tires in the rear position. The crime occurred in the early summer when snow tires have usually been removed, making a car with snow tires at this time of year all the more unique and noticeable. Indeed, 24 hours later an alert detective called into the crime lab. He had noticed a small Rambler in a driveway with Ward's Traction Grip snow tires in the rear. Because the front tire identification was new evidence, the crime lab officer asked what was on the front. The detective said, "I've never heard of it before, but they're Jetzon Gemini IIs." A vehicle registration check quickly determined the owner of the vehicle.

When the home of the vehicle owner was entered by the police, he was found dead with a revolver next to him—apparently a suicide because his home had been under surveillance. Test impressions made of all tires on the vehicle confirmed that the suspect's vehicle had been used in the crime. (Figure 10.28). No trial was necessary.

# Test Tire Impressions 11

If the tires on a suspect's vehicle visually appear to be similar to a crime scene imprint, test impressions of the suspect's tires should be prepared. The comparison and identification procedure for tire footprint impressions employs many of the same basic procedures used with fingerprint impressions. This chapter describes one system used for preparing tire test impressions.

Even if a crime scene imprint is recorded in a soft, pliable substance to display all characteristics most clearly, the tire for the test impression should be rolled over a firm board. (I have tried reconstructing a substrate similar to that at the crime scene for comparison, but that only adds another variable and conceals many accidental characteristics that might otherwise be visible.)

Test impressions are nondestructive and may be repeated if necessary. They are most easily prepared inside a garage and out of the wind and weather, but an outside location is fine on a nice day. Allow about a two-vehicle length of smooth, hard, level surface on which to drive the test tires. Tires must be loaded and inflated.

## Materials Needed for Making Test Impressions

The following materials will be needed to make test tire print impressions. Materials can be purchased at art supply stores.

**POSTER BOARD (WHITE HOT PRESS, 14-PLY)**

☐ The thick poster board is necessary to avoid imprinting the surface below.

□  The rigidity of the poster board avoids squirming and contraction as loaded tire is rolled over it.

□  Illustration board is very satisfactory, but it is more costly than poster board.

□  White poster board is most readily available, but a light contrasting color is satisfactory.

□  Smooth "Hot Press" is a more precise surface than the rougher "Cold Press" type, and it requires less ink.

**INK**

□  Fingerprint Black Ink (4 oz. tube). Available from Lightning Power Company Inc., 1230 Hoyt Street, S.E., Salem, OR 97302-2121 (800-852-0300). Squeeze directly on the poster board and spread evenly with an ink roller.

□  New Era FR Black Ink (1 lb. can), Product Code 101K08190. Available from Braden Sutphin Ink Company, 3650 East 93rd Street, Cleveland, Ohio 44105 (800-362-9101). Spatula directly onto poster board.

Note: Most other inks do not imprint well or have a good shelf life.

**SPATULA**

□  Used to spread ink on the poster board when preparing the ink pad.

**INK ROLLER (BRAYER)**

□  Used to smooth out ink film over entire ink pad surface.

**WAX CRAYON**

□  Use a light color to contrast with the black tire. Children's Crayola crayons are quite satisfactory.

**PEN**

□  Used to record test information data.

**CLEANING SOLUTION**

□  Mineral spirits (paint thinner) will clean tools and hands after completion.

*Step 1:* Cut poster board into approximately 10″ strips, or wider for wide tires. Tape ends together on back side. The total board length should exceed the tire circumference—three 40″-long boards will handle any passenger tire. One full-circumference board is for the ink pad; the other full-circumference boards are for test impressions. See Figure 11.1.

*Step 2:* Clean surface dirt and debris from the tire only if it is very dirty. Do not dislodge stones wedged in tread grooves.

*Step 3:* Place a small amount of ink on the poster board to prepare an ink pad. Spread the ink around with the ink roller, covering the entire board. Be careful not to put too much ink on—just get board black. If excess ink is used, it will run down into the grooves and sipes and give a blotted imprint. Conversely, ink should not be left to dry out. The ink pad will need to be freshened every few imprints dependent on weather conditions.

*Step 4:* Now one person can slowly drive or push the vehicle over the ink pad that has been positioned directly in front of or behind the test tire by another person. This will consistently ink the com-

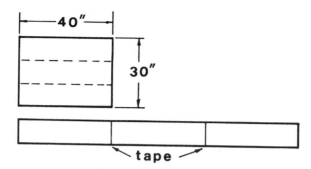

**Figure 11.1.** Poster board may be cut into convenient lengths for test impressions.

plete tread so that it is ready to roll onto a clean white board of the same length.

*Step 5:* Roll the inked tire a few inches onto the clean board, stop, and use the wax crayon to mark a radial line on the tire sidewall at 6 o'clock. Also mark the same relative starting point on the poster board. Now slowly roll down the board for one full revolution, until the crayon line returns to the 6 o'clock position. Stop, then mark the same relative point on the board. Roll off board and remove. *Caution:* To avoid an overlapping second tire imprint, it may be necessary to pull the long cardboard imprint away before the trailing tire reaches it.

*Step 6:* Identify the test impressions with the following information:
Investigator's name
Date
Tire design name and size
Tire position—e.g., RF (right front)
Outside or white side
DOT serial number and/or mold number

Note that to view the serial number and/or mold number it will probably be necessary to crawl under the vehicle with a flashlight and look at the back side of the tire near the rim. See Chapter 5 for information that may be learned from the serial number.

*Step 7:* Follow the procedure above for all test impressions required. Before marking pitch lengths directly on test impressions, let ink impressions dry.

The inked test impression shown in Figure 11.2 was made by a Firestone Supreme design as shown in Figure 11.3.

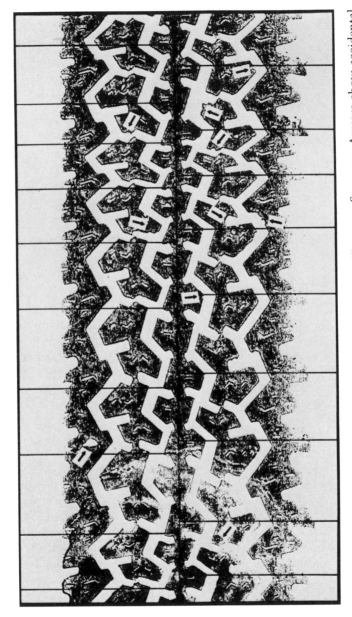

**Figure 11.2.** Part of an inked test impression made from a Firestone Supreme. Arrows show accidental characteristics.

**Figure 11.3.** Firestone Supreme. *(Courtesy of Firestone Tire & Rubber Co.)*

If the spare tire is suspect, a test impression should be prepared after mounting the spare on the vehicle.

Do not be too concerned if the tires are no longer on the suspect's vehicle. Mount them on a similar vehicle with rated inflation pressure. The tread elements will not change significantly with air pressure or load variations.

# Tire Noise Treatments 12

*All passenger tires manufactured today use some form of noise treatment or pitch sequencing, as it is also called, to reduce tire-emitted road noise.*

(Nause 1987)

A tire's noise treatment—that is, the arrangement of different pitch lengths of the elements around the circumference of a tire's tread—can be a major clue for an investigator in making a positive identification.

As the tire rolls, the many tread elements and sipes necessary for traction interact with the road surface texture to create *tire noise*. The size, the sequencing of pitch lengths, and the angles of the tread elements determine the intensity, tonality, and persistence of the noise generated. Noise level increases with speed, load, the amount of wear, the smoothness of the road, and wet or dry conditions. If the tread elements were held consistent, the noise spectrum would yield a definite fundamental frequency. The tire would be very "tonal." To minimize tire noise, the sequencing of pitch lengths is varied around the circumference of the tire. The pitches may also be staggered laterally across the tread face.

The computer is today's drawing board for the tire designer. It can help determine the optimum sequence of pitches. Using the computer, the designer can not only construct the design, but also generate the pitch sequence and analyze the frequencies of a tread pattern.

A basic zig-zag type groove in a tire tread has pitches as shown in Figure 12.1. Pitches in this tread pattern are defined as: *S*, small; *M*, medium; and *L*, large. Some designs have very simple methods of reducing tread noise and are generally used with retreads, older

**Figure 12.1.**  Partial noise treatment with pitches designated as: *S*, small; *M*, medium; and *L*, large.

passenger tread patterns, or truck tires. They might have a simple variation of small, medium, and large pitches repeated around the full circumference of the tire, as shown in Figure 12.2.

In Figure 12.3 the noise treatment is slightly more complex. Model A has pitches varying in length from a small 1 to a large 8. Model B is the reverse. The model sequence shows two repeating models. The top half of the mold is generally the whitewall side. A tire manufacturer's tread drawing will always show a diagram of the pitch sequence.

The models on one side of the tread do not always line up exactly with the models on the other side. This offset may be designed as part of the noise treatment, to stabilize tread elements, or just for appearance. In the manufacturing process, it is not uncommon for tires produced from one mold to have a different offset from tires of another mold. One mold half might be offset as much as one-tenth of an inch in either direction without being detected in production. This can be a clue for an investigator in determining "mold vs. mold" with a specific tire design.

### Case Study 12.1

Sometimes findings even exonerate a suspect.

I was involved in a Nottingham, Pennsylvania, homicide case where mold offset was a major clue in solving tire identity. The Pennsylvania State Police brought four Firestone Deluxe Champion tires to my office for examination. The tires had been mounted on a suspect's vehicle, which had been found by the road near the location of a murder that had occurred the previous night.

**Figure 12.2.**  Repeating model sequence of noise treatment for full circumference of tire.

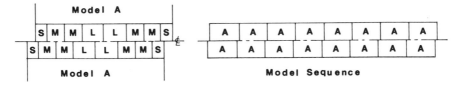

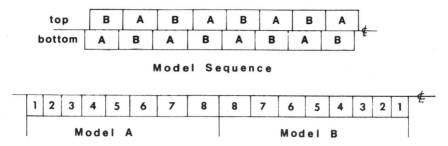

Figure 12.3.  A more complex noise treatment: two models repeating four times in the circumference.

The police also had an excellent photograph of a Deluxe Champion tire imprint (Figure 12.4) taken at the scene of the homicide.

Careful examination revealed that three of the tires could be eliminated because they had different wear patterns from those shown in the crime scene imprint. The fourth tire had similar general accidental characteristics, but the crime scene imprint clearly showed a different offset.

**Figure 12.4.**  Firestone Deluxe Champion tire imprint. (*Courtesy of Capt. James Sagans, Pennsylvania State Police*)

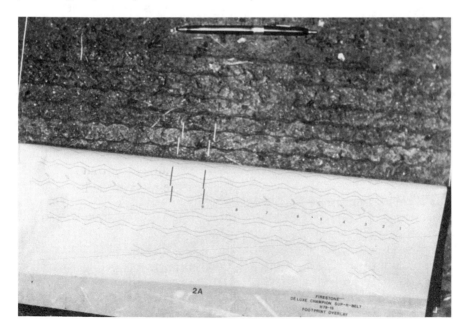

The man the police had in custody said, "I was out stealing cars that night, not murdering." The imprint proved he was probably telling the truth. Captain James Sagans of the Pennsylvania State Police later stated: "Even though the tire footprints did not match, the information and findings gained were such that it reinforced our case and aided our investigation, culminating in several arrests, five of which were for murder."

Computer technology has made possible very complex noise treatments to quiet today's aggressive tire designs. Tires produced often have many different pitch lengths and sequences that may not repeat around the total circumference of the tire. This process is costly, requiring different models around the full circumference. All current O.E.-type passenger tires have complex noise treatments.

The more complicated the noise treatment, the easier it will be for the experienced investigator to make a positive identification. After the exact sequence of pitches is discovered, the accidental characteristics can be reviewed. *Caution:* Some manufacturers change the noise treatment sequence slightly for different-size tires of the same design. When requesting tread drawings, specify the size if possible. This is an additional reason for confirming noise treatment by means of a tread drawing.

The example in Figure 12.5 has only a very short imprint, but the investigator who understands pitch sequences can get more than enough information to find an exact location. (Of course, longer sections of tire imprints are definitely desirable.)

Now compare the tire imprint, shown in Figure 12.5, that has the pitches defined with white numbers with the tread drawing pitch sequence in Figure 12.6. There is only one place that correlates exactly. Can you find it? Remember, the tread drawing pitch sequence is in the reverse direction of the tire imprint. (*Answer:* The sequence of the first three pitches in Figure 12.6, when reversed, exactly fits the tire imprint in Figure 12.5.)

If tread drawings cannot be obtained, it takes a trained eye and much study to distinguish where pitches start or end. With successive measurements, the code can be broken, but I feel most confident if tread drawings are available.

If a tire manufacturer is sensitive about furnishing a tread drawing, the examiner might ask for only the tire tread sequence (Figure 12.7). This is all that is needed to establish the pitch sequence.

It is interesting to note a slight variation between Figure 12.7 and Figure 12.8, an initial tire photograph. This design was first manufac-

**Figure 12.5.** Short tire imprint showing unique sequence of pitch lengths.

Tire Imprint

tured with "landlocked" or "contained" sipes in all the tread elements, but later it was found to be noisy. The solution was to vent each sipe to the outer edge of the tread elements. The molds were modified and the drawings reflect this variation. *Warning:* Molds may be changed slightly from the picture seen in the *Tread Design Guide.* If in doubt, check with the manufacturer. The variation observed might be a "mold vs. mold" characteristic.

**Figure 12.6.** Tread drawing of noise treatment allows the investigator to find one exact location of pitches.

TOP — 6 5 5 6 3 5 1 3 4 6 2 4 4 6 4 6 3 5 1 3 5 7 5 7 3 5 2 4 1 3 5 7 3 5 2 4 1 3 5 7 3 5 2 4 2 4 1 3 4 6

BOTTOM 4 7 2 6 4 5 1 2 7 3 5 4 2 6 7 5 2 1 1 6 4 2 5 7 2 4 5 6 4 1 7 3 3 3 5 4 4 1 3 3 4 5 5 5 3 3 3 4 6 5

64 PITCHES
15-(7)'S   34-(9)'S   15-(11)'S

TIRE TREAD SEQUENCE
P185/70R14 Arriva

Clockwise relative to the non-serial side.

7-7-9-9-11-11-9-9-9-7-9-11-9-9-9-7-7-7-9-9-9-11-
11-11-9-9-9-7-7-9-9-11-11-9-9-9-7-9-11-9-9-9-7-
7-9-9-11-11-9-9-7-7-7-7-9-9-9-9-11-11-11-11-9-9

**Figure 12.7.** Tire tread sequence of pitches helps investigator break code. (*Courtesy of Goodyear Tire & Rubber Co.*)

**Figure 12.8.** Initial tire photographs showing "land locked" sipes. (*Courtesy of Goodyear Tire & Rubber Co.*)

## Tread Wear Indicators and Noise Treatment

Figure 12.7 shows a T.W.I., or tread wear indicator, in the number 9 pitch. More information would be needed to describe all the locations around the circumference. All tires approved by the U.S. Department of Transportation have tread wear indicators (see Figure 12.9). A tread wear indicator is a raised portion at the base of the tread groove that appears locally smooth when the tread is worn to one-sixteenth of an inch above the base of the groove—indicating that it is time to remove the tire from service. Tires of 12-inch rim diameter or more have at least six indicators.

**Figure 12.9.** Schematic tread showing tread wear indicator.

**Figure 12.10.** Typical plaster model showing exact design that will be repeated in all resultant molds. (*Courtesy of Firestone Tire & Rubber Co.*)

Tire molds are generally precision cast from plaster models. Tread wear indicators are cast into master models in exact locations, making all molds of this process identical (see Figure 12.10). However, if only a few molds per size are required, it may be more economical to engrave each mold individually. This may account for inconsistencies in the location of tread wear indicators with respect to noise treatment. The result is "mold vs. mold" variations. Case Study 14.2, in Chapter 14 shows how significant observing a tread wear indicator can be in an actual case. Tread wear indicators are most obvious in very worn tire imprints.

# Using Tire Tread Drawings 13

*Tires come in a multiplicity of patterns depending on types of service conditions. Some designs are highly complex and contain as many as 9,000 gripping edges.*

(Kovac 1978)

Tire drawings help investigators visualize a new or worn design with or without a suspect's tire.

It is not always possible to obtain a new tire of the same design and size to analyze. This chapter acquaints the investigator with drawings used for the manufacturing of tires. Understanding tire groove cross-sectional shapes can be very useful when trying to determine the rate of wear and why a tread pattern changes in appearance.

## Rate of Wear

For example, if the tire imprint to be examined looked like that in Figure 13.1, a review of a portion of the manufacturer's tread drawing for that tire (Figure 13.2) might well give a fairly accurate indication of the amount of wear. (*Note:* Information that is not relevant has been omitted from this typical drawing. Dimensions are usually given in hundredths of an inch.)

The tire that made the imprint in Figure 13.1 was worn slightly less than half the total skid depth. Can you see why? After studying the highlighted tread drawing (Figure 13.3) the answer should be apparent: Notice that the notches in the center rib are completely eliminated in the worn tire imprint; therefore, the center of the tire is worn more than 0.20 inches, as defined in the notch section D-E. Also notice that

**Figure 13.1.**   Typical worn tire imprint rendering.

**Figure 13.2.**   A portion of a typical manufacturer's tread drawing used to determine depths in Figure 13.1.

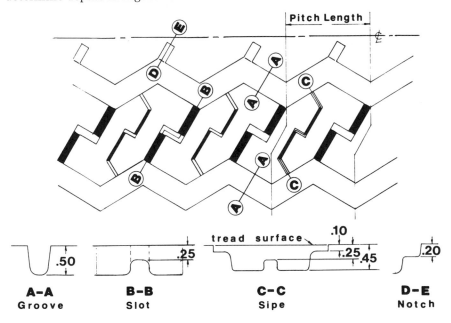

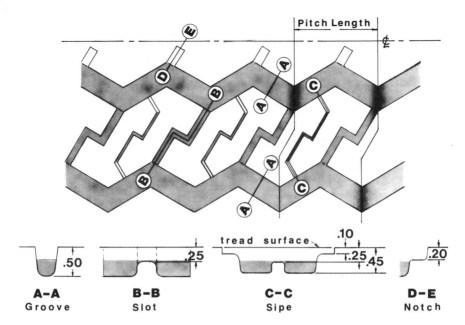

**Figure 13.3.** Highlighted tread drawing graphically showing wear level of Figure 13.1.

the center tie bars of slot B-B and sipe C-C are not yet exposed in the imprint; therefore, that rib is not yet half worn. If the tire were worn more than 0.25 inches, the center portion of the slots and sipes would not leave any raised embossment. Groove section A-A gives little information about wear.

The depth of grooves in one location of a tire may differ from another. Irregular rib wear may become obvious when studied with the aid of tread drawings, and be an important factor in general accidental wear characteristics.

## Determining Tire Rib Variations

Most tire sizes are proportionately larger or smaller than a base size design. Rib widths and pitch lengths will vary to fit the tread width or tire circumference, but for a variety of reasons the tire designer may need to reduce the number of ribs on small sizes. For example, a basic seven-rib design, when proportioned to a narrow width, may "squiggle." "Squiggle" occurs when the circumferential tire rib spacing corresponds to the spacing of longitudinal grooves that are sometimes ground into highways for improved wet traction. These highway grooves are designed to be three-quarters of an inch apart. Tire designers try to avoid this spacing of ribs that may result in "squiggle" or "groove wander" because most tires approved by O.E. accounts must pass a squiggle test.

Tire tread drawings are useful for determining pitches and pitch sequence. Knowing the approximate nonskid depths and the location of tie bars is also advantageous, because most tire imprints are made by worn tires that have changed from their new appearance.

## Dimensions

Dimensions shown on tread drawings will not be exactly the same as the dimensions in the tire imprints. First, it should always be determined whether a drawing is a tread drawing or a mold drawing, because mold groove shapes change when an inflated tire expands, and loaded tire grooves will compress when deflected on the varying road surface.

A mold drawing may be a reverse image of the tire imprint. The drawing may state: "Layout is for design at face of tire and looking at the tire." Also, mold groove width dimensions will not necessarily be the same as those for the inflated tire. Grooves may open or close, based on tire construction, inflation, or other variables, but the tire groove depths will not change significantly from mold to tire.

# What Can Be Learned When You Do Have a Suspect's Tire

# 14

*Areas on the suspect tire which could have made the crime scene impression can be accurately determined and then Accidental Characteristics, if present, can be located with the same degree of accuracy.*

(Nause 1987)

This chapter explains the procedure after obtaining a suspect's vehicle or tires (Figure 14.1). The preliminary procedure to follow when the investigator does have the suspect's vehicle is the same as that for cases where the suspect's vehicle is not available (see Chapter 10). If starting from the beginning, however, refer to Chapter 10 for the complete procedure.

## Prepare an Inked Test Impression

Chapter 11 describes how to prepare test impressions. All tires on the suspect's vehicle should be imprinted, even the spare.

## Define Pitch Lengths on Test Impressions

If the examiner has received tread drawings from the manufacturer, these will be very useful at this point (see Figure 14.2). The sequence of pitches shown on the tread drawing can now be transferred to the test impressions (Figure 14.3). Mark all pitch lines and label them. If you are not confident about marking directly on the test impression, make a practice overlay. A final clear plastic overlay with contrasting colors is also effective.

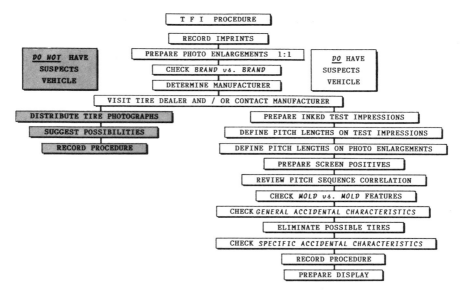

**Figure 14.1.**  Tire imprint identification procedure (when suspect's tire *is* available).

If tread drawings cannot be obtained, try to determine the sequence of pitches from measurements. It may not be exactly the same system the manufacturer used, and it is not easy to do, but it is a way to locate a consistent sequence of pitches quickly.

## Define Pitch Lengths on Photo Enlargement

Now define a few of the pitches on the full-size crime scene photograph, using a procedure similiar to that used on the test impression (see Figure 14.4). Defining the pitch lengths makes comparison easier. Narrow contrasting tape or ink lines are effective and easy to apply to photographs. A drawing triangle will ensure perpendicular lines from the center.

## Prepare Screen Positives

As described in Chapter 7, a continuous tone transparency should be made. These screen positives are made directly from a full-size black-and-white crime scene photograph. They may be made from the actual picture taken at the scene or from a photograph of the crime scene casting. Remember, a screen positive made from a photograph of a casting will be turned over when compared with a test imprint. The

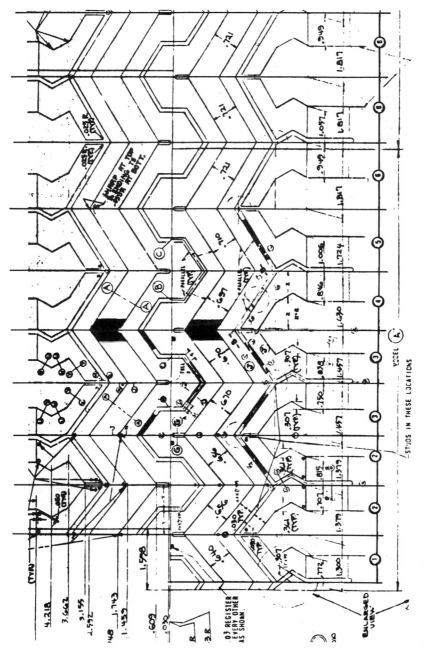

**Figure 14.2.** Portion of manufacturer's tread drawing for an understanding of the complex sequence of pitches. (*Courtesy of Firestone Tire & Rubber Co.*)

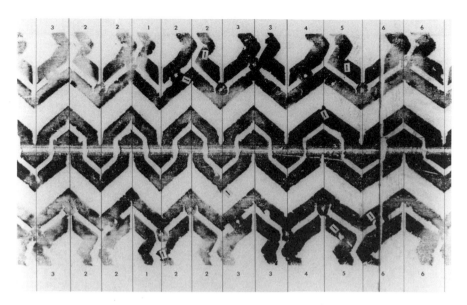

**Figure 14.3.** Test impression pitch sequence defined on test impression with understanding of the tread drawings. *(Courtesy of Luis Bautista, Deputy Sheriff, Riverside County, Indio, Calif.)*

**Figure 14.4.** Pitch sequence defined on crime scene photograph with understanding of the tread drawings. *(Courtesy of David S. W. Pong, Riverside County Sheriff, Indio, Calif.)*

**Figure 14.5.** Screen positive of crime scene photograph to be used as overlay. *(Courtesy of David S. W. Pong, Riverside County Sheriff, Indio, Calif.)*

scale in the picture will serve as a reminder of which side is up. This screen positive will later be used as an overlay when comparing the crime scene photograph with the test impression (see Figure 14.5).

## Review Pitch Sequence Correlation

Check the sequence of pitches on the full-size photograph for correlation with any sequence of pitches on the test impression. More than one sequence may be repeated around the tire—check for this. The transparency can now be put over the places where the pitch sequence is the same (see Figure 14.6).

The examiner's first question might be: "Do I have the transparency turned the right way?" or "Does the outside of the crime scene imprint correlate with the outside of the test impression?" Tires are generally symmetrical, so if the photograph of the crime scene was originally identified with the "outside" this procedure is less difficult.

## Check "Mold vs. Mold" Features

Assuming that the questioned tire design, size, and sequence of pitches is consistent, now check the "mold vs. mold" features. Examiners should resist the temptation to go directly to the specific accidental

**Figure 14.6.** Typical screen positive overlayed on test impression. *(Courtesy of L. A. Nause, RCMP)*

characteristics. Follow the procedure, and don't jump to conclusions. A case in point is Case Study 12.1, where mold offset exonerated a suspect.

## Check General Accidental Characteristics

General accidental characteristics might be the reason that one location of the transparency may fit better than all others. Focus on the sequence that fits best. If more than one tire is recorded at the crime scene, the odds of another vehicle having the same combination of tires *and* the same general accidental characteristics is extremely remote.

## Eliminate Possible Tires

If a suspect vehicle has more than one tire of the same design, it may be time to eliminate suspect tires. Check all test impressions. Even if it is obvious that only one tire has similar general accidental characteristics, this will broaden the examiner's knowledge and will ultimately show the jury how complete the examination was. Determination of why a tire of the same design *could not* have made the crime scene imprint is also very valuable evidence (see Case Study 14.2 in this chapter). General accidental characteristics alone may make it possible to eliminate all tires except one. This helps establish the significance of a general accidental characteristic. A good example of this is Case Study 16.3, in Chapter 16.

## Check Specific Accidental Characteristics

If the general accidental characteristics of one exact location of the test imprint correlate with those of the crime scene imprint, look for *specific* accidental characteristics. These characteristics will be most visible in the test impression, but the examiner is less subject to seeing what he or she wants to see if the review for specific accidental characteristics is made first in the crime scene imprint and then in the test impression. If one characteristic looks promising, move the screen positive over the test impression to confirm. For contrast in the area being studied, I often slide a white paper beneath the screen positive.

Avoid using dimensional measurements when comparing evidence. The examiner is generally studying a crime scene imprint made in a soft substance by a vehicle that was in a hurry to leave the scene, and possibly months prior to preparing the test impression. The controlled test impression, however, is made on a hard, smooth surface, and the tire is moved slowly to imprint every current detail. Even with a scale placed as accurately as possible on the tread surface, there will be slight graduated discrepancies in the one-to-one enlargement. Also, the paper used for the enlargement may shrink slightly.

It should be remembered that when a tire under load rolls over an irregular surface it is pushed in by the bumps and squeezed down into the depressions. A tire rolling over a bump does not just roll over it—it rolls around it. The tread bends around the bump, and the sidewalls bulge out (Figure 14.7). Even on a "smooth" crime scene imprint the tread surface distorts as the tire rolls over the hundreds of depressions, allowing the tire to develop traction to change the speed and direction of the vehicle (Figure 14.8.)

In a controlled experiment I determined that the total length of the one-to-one scale crime scene imprint may differ slightly from the test impression. For this reason, the examiners should direct their attention to the shape of each specific accidental characteristic within each individual tread element. Check specific accidental characteristics one tread element at a time. Many characteristics will remain for a long period of time. (See Case Study 14.1 in this chapter.)

After finding one specific accidental characteristic, look for more—it gets easier. List each one. Place arrows on the test impression that correspond to arrows on the crime scene photograph. Transfer-type arrows or numbers and ink lines may be applied to point out specific accidental characteristics (Figure 14.9).

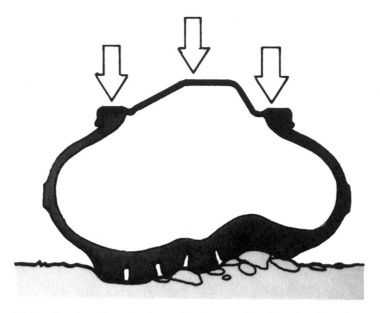

**Figure 14.7.** Section showing how the tire tread under a load bends around a bump.

**Figure 14.8.** Side view showing how the tread surface distorts.

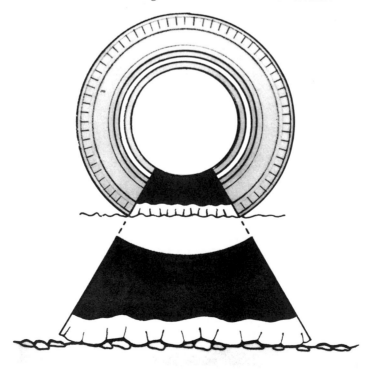

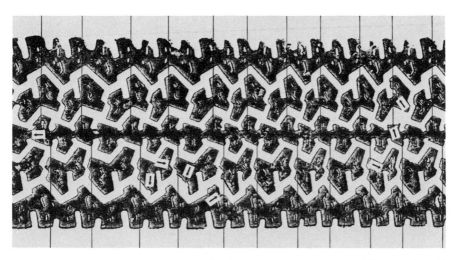

**Figure 14.9.** Test impression with arrows pointing to specific accidental characteristics.

### Case Study 14.1

In this unique case, two Canadian policemen from Winnipeg, Manitoba, Barry Nielsen and Jerry Stolar, were accused in 1983 of murdering the brother-in-law of one. The victim was beaten to death after apparently being intercepted on his way to work late at night. A puddle of the victim's blood was left at the scene, and a barefoot print and tire print were found at the scene—both in the blood of the victim. A North Carolina professor of anthropology and a forensic scientist from Scotland Yard's crime laboratory examined the barefoot print evidence. They later testified that the barefoot print at the scene was consistent with the suspect Nielsen's footprint.

I was asked to help compare the suspect's tires with photographs taken of the bloody tire imprints from the crime scene. Photography was obviously the best way to record the tire imprint on the highway. Casting was not possible, and removing a section of the road surface to take to the laboratory would be impractical.

It was theorized that the barefoot suspect stepped in the blood of the victim and then loaded the body into his station wagon to be transported to a pre-dug grave. The suspects, Nielsen and Stolar, then drove over the puddle of blood with the right rear tire, so when the tire entered the smooth highway it carried fresh blood with it. Imprints were visible at every revolution for 200 feet (see Figures 14.10 and 14.11). As noted by the investigator, imprint 4 was particularly distinct (see Figure 14.12) and used for the

**Figure 14.10.** Winnipeg case general crime scene photographs of bloody tire imprints visible at every revolution—1. *(Courtesy of R. L. Thompson, Identification Section, Winnipeg Police Dept., Manitoba, Canada)*

majority of my comparisons with the test impression (see Figure 14.13).

Eight months after the crime, the investigating officer secured the suspect's vehicle. Even though the investigator, R. L. Thompson, was particularly suspicious of the right rear tire, I asked for test impressions of all tires. I was also given tread drawings of this

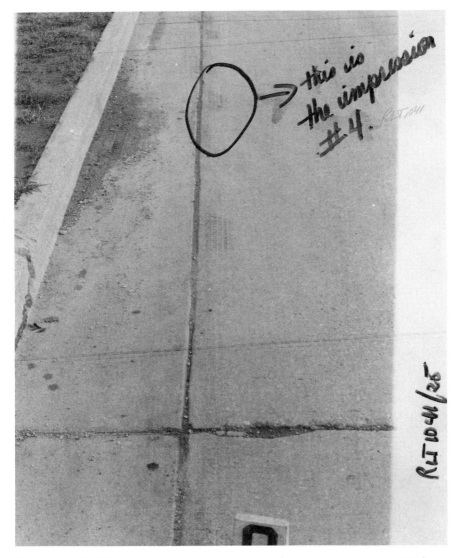

**Figure 14.11.** Winnipeg case crime scene showing impression #4 location. *(Courtesy of R. L. Thompson, Identification Section, Winnipeg Police Dept., Manitoba, Canada)*

design, which was manufactured by Seiberling of Canada. Screen positives were also furnished. Within a day of receiving this material, I prepared a report stating that the left front, right front, and left rear tires, all of the same design and size, *did not* correlate with the crime scene.

With the aid of the tread drawing, I reviewed the various pitch

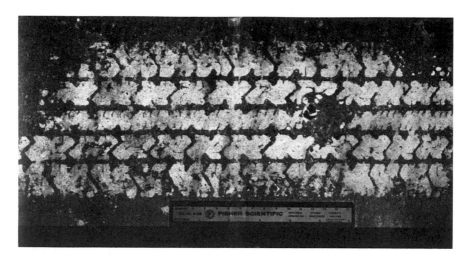

**Figure 14.12.** Imprint #4 in Winnipeg case. *(Courtesy of R. L. Thompson, Identification Section, Winnipeg Police Dept., Manitoba, Canada)*

lengths and noise treatment sequence of the right rear test impression (Figure 14.13). The sequence of pitches repeated three times in the full circumference. After studying all three sections, I found one sequence that had corresponding general accidental characteristics. Further study revealed nine specific accidental characteristics. This made it possible to make a positive identification.

It is significant that in this case, involving both tire "footprint" identification and the suspect's actual "footprint," a positive identification could be made with the bloody tire imprint while

**Figure 14.13.** Right rear test impression used to compare with imprint #4 in Winnipeg case. *(Courtesy of R. L. Thompson, Identification Section, Winnipeg Police Dept., Manitoba, Canada)*

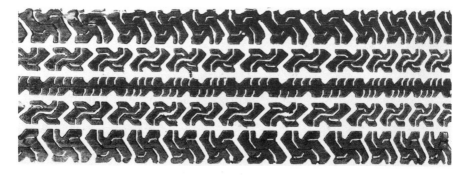

the person's "footprint" identification was only "consistent." It should also be noted that the specific accidental characteristics found eight months later on the right rear tire were still visible. The tires had not been rotated. This shows that tire evidence is not nearly as fragile as is often assumed. Many specific accidental characteristics remain for thousands of miles of tread wear.

### Case Study 14.2

In a 1981 Akron, Ohio, murder case (*Summit County v. Gilbert*), tire tracks were the key to identifying the murderer. Three days after the murder, Detective Ron Stinson from the Akron Police Department visited my office. He gave me a small Polaroid photograph of a plaster casting made outside a Stop-n-Go store (Figure 14.14). The tire had run off the paved surface and made a good imprint. A trail of blood from the abducted clerk led to the specific tire tracks that were cast. The detective wanted to know the tire design name and manufacturer. There were no suspects.

Within 10 hours I could tell the detective that the imprint was made by a Duralon DS Premium tire, manufactured by Dayton. I provided him with a three-quarter view photograph of this tire

**Figure 14.14.** Polaroid photograph of casting from Akron crime scene. *(Courtesy of Fredric L. Zuch, Assistant Prosecuting Attorney, Akron, Ohio)*

**Figure 14.15.** Three-quarter view photograph of Duralon DS Premium tire. *(Courtesy of Firestone Tire & Rubber Co.)*

(Figure 14.15). Copies of the photo were circulated to other investigators.

The next week, Detective Stinson and an assistant were sent to a suspect's home. Because Stinson was alert to my suggestion of a Duralon DS Premium tire, the first thing he did was check a vehicle in the carport. The car had Duralons on the rear. The owner was questioned, tried to run away, but was subsequently taken into custody. Coincidentally, another suspect questioned also had Duralon DS Premium tires on his van, but they were larger.

The suspect, Gilbert, maintained his innocence, so the local Bureau of Criminal Investigation asked for my assistance in identifying the evidence. A casting had also been made of a tire imprint found near the dead girl's body, so I had photographs taken of each casting: casting B near the body (Figure 14.16) and casting A outside the store (Figure 14.17). For scale, a ruler was placed at approximately the surface level of the tread. Oblique lighting was used to highlight features. Actual-size 1 : 1 enlargements were prepared, and both a screen positive and a screen negative were made of each. (Screen positives are most useful when overlaying inked test impressions. Screen negatives may be used to overlay the actual tire, but they are of little value in the investigative process.)

The next step was to prepare test impressions from the two rear tires. Significant portions of these impressions are shown in Figures 14.18 and 14.19. Figure 14.18 was the section 1 from the right rear tire that I later found to be consistent with casting B;

**Figure 14.16.** Cast B taken from near body at Akron crime scene. *(Courtesy of Fredric L. Zuch, Assistant Prosecuting Attorney, Akron, Ohio)*

**Figure 14.17.** Cast A taken outside store near Akron crime scene. *(Courtesy of Fredric L. Zuch, Assistant Prosecuting Attorney, Akron, Ohio)*

**Figure 14.18.** Portion of test impression #1 from right rear tire of suspect's vehicle in Akron case.

Figure 14.19 was the section from the right rear tire that I later found to be a positive identification with casting A. The front tires were a different brand and did not leave imprints. Because the abduction scene casting indicated the presence of a tread wear indicator, I marked all tread wear indicators with a wax crayon on the tire sidewall and transferred that location to the test impressions.

The elimination process became easier when I discovered that the left rear tire came from a different mold than the right rear. This was first observed when examining the tread wear indicator in relation to the noise treatment. Later, when checking the serial

**Figure 14.19.** Portion of test impression #2 from right rear tire of suspect's vehicle in Akron case.

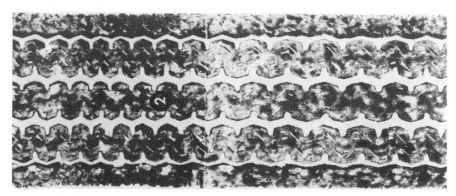

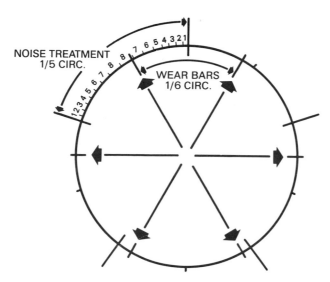

**Figure 14.20.** Schematic of noise treatment/wear bar orientation for right rear tire in Akron case.

numbers, it was apparent that even though the tires were produced from different molds they had been manufactured in the same week (see end of Chapter 12 on tread wear indicators and noise treatment).

The tread wear indicators or wear bar locations can best be described by a diagram showing noise treatment / wear bar orientation (Figure 14.20). Only a few molds were made for this size Duralon tire, so it was more economical to engrave each mold instead of casting the molds. The wear bars in these engraved molds were randomly located—each mold was different. Casting molds, however, are typically identical, although even when molds are cast the tread wear indicators may be added later by hand-stamping or cutting.

The diagram in Figure 14.20 was made as a display for the trial to help explain the unique position each wear bar had in relationship to the noise treatment. The noise treatment repeats five times around the circumference. The equally spaced wear bars repeat six times around the circumference. Because the noise treatment repeats five times, I studied each of the five segments of corresponding pitches for correlation. One section was found to fit best.

With these general accidental characteristics established, I was able to focus on one sequence of pitches, where I discovered many *specific* accidental characteristics. The last step in this examination was to identify all the specific accidental characteristics on the *actual tire*. Contrasting tape defined the area; white adhesive-backed arrows highlighted specific points. I find that an actual tire is a good graphic tool for testifying in court, although sometimes photographic enlargements are better if you are trying to show the jury specific accidental characteristics that are small in size.

This was an exciting case to present, and my first experience testifying. I found it took one-and-a-half days of testimony to educate the jury about the specific features present. All the background I had in tire design helped me clarify, in laymen's terms, the information relevant to this case. The case was solved and the killer was convicted, in good part because of the testimony about the tire imprints.

This case encompassed much of what has been discussed in the previous chapters. It was important to convey to the jury the basic mechanics of the tire tread (Chapter 2). Tire sales and manufacturing issues (Chapter 3) were involved. The distinctive wear patterns of tires (Chapter 4) were important. Information about the tire sidewalls (Chapter 5) confirmed molding identification. The crime scene (Chapter 6) was clearly established. Photographing tire impressions and castings and preparing screen positives (Chapter 7) were essential for analysis. Wheelbase and tire tread stance measurements (Chapter 8) were not available, but tire imprint identification standards (Chapter 9) helped the detectives recognize the significance of one suspect's tire imprint. The police found out what could be learned if a suspect's vehicle is not available (see Chapter 10). I instructed the detective on how to prepare test impressions (Chapter 11). An understanding of tire noise treatments and the tread wear indicators (Chapter 12) helped me find specific accidental characteristics. And tire drawings (Chapter 13) directed my attention to the worn sipe pattern variations. This all resulted in the procedure outlining what to do if you do have a suspect's vehicle (Chapter 14). The information in all the chapters in this book will help the tire investigator. It would be unfortunate to try shortcutting the process to come to a quick conclusion.

# One Case, From Beginning to End

# 15

*The scope of a complete examination consists of two main functions: first, the recovery process, which includes the discovery and preservation of latent prints, and second, the identification process, which involves evaluations, comparisons, and findings related to the recovered impression.*

(Grieve 1988)

In this chapter we shall see how many features of tire imprint identification can be encompassed in a single case (*New Jersey v. Koedatich*, 1985), in which I was asked to help. This case started with a letter from Detective Jeffrey Muraski of the New Jersey State Police. His department was investigating a homicide in which the victim was forced off the road, abducted, and later murdered.

At the scene of the abduction, investigators had found a tire impression that they believed the perpetrator's vehicle had made. Muraski asked if I would help identify the vehicle from the casting (Figure 15.1). I was also given a poorly lighted color photograph of the crime scene impression (Figure 15.2). The impression was similar to the well-known Firestone Town & Country design, but possibly a variation similar to nearly 35 different passenger and retread snow tires listed in the 1973 *Tread Design Guide*. I listed all possibilities; one was a Seiberling Snow Power Radial (Figure 15.3).

Seven months later James Koedatich was arrested for the abduction and murder of Deirdre O'Brien. His rear tires were HR78-15 Seiberling Snow Power radials. Test impressions were made of all tires. It was obvious that the general accidental characteristics of the left rear tire test impression (see Figure 15.4), had not made the impression cast at

**Figure 15.1.** Casting of tire impression in New Jersey case. *(Courtesy of Charles E. Waldron, New Jersey State Division of Criminal Justice)*

**Figure 15.2.** Photograph of crime scene impression. *(Courtesy of Charles E. Waldron, New Jersey State Division of Criminal Justice)*

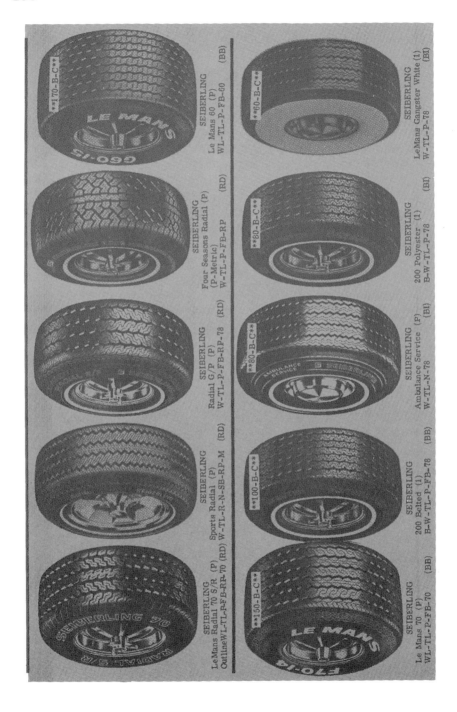

**SEIBERLING**
Le Mans 60 (P)
WL-TL-P-FB-60 (BB)

**SEIBERLING**
Four Seasons Radial (P)
(P-Metric)
W-TL-P-FB-RP (RD)

**SEIBERLING**
Radial G/P (P)
W-TL-P-FB-RP-78 (RD)

**SEIBERLING**
Sports Radial (P)
W-TL-R-N-SB-RP-M (RD)

**SEIBERLING**
LeMans Radial 70 S/R (P)
OutlineWL-TL-R-FB-RP-70 (RD)

**SEIBERLING**
LeMans Gangster White (1)
W-TL-P-FB-78 (BI)

**SEIBERLING**
200 Polyester (1)
B-W-TL-P-78 (BI)

**SEIBERLING**
Ambulance Service (P)
W-TL-N-78 (BI)

**SEIBERLING**
200 Belted (1)
B-W-TL-P-FB-78 (BB)

**SEIBERLING**
Le Mans 70 (P)
WL-TL-P-FB-70 (BB)

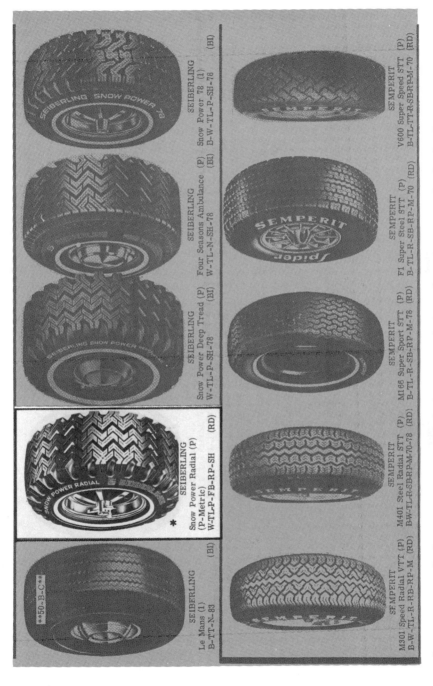

**Figure 15.3.** Seiberling Snow Power Radial. *(Courtesy of Al Snyder, editor, Tire Guides Inc.)*

**Figure 15.4.** Test impression of suspect's left rear tire in New Jersey case. *(Courtesy of Charles E. Waldron, New Jersey State Division of Criminal Justice)*

the crime scene, because the short test impression of the same sequence of pitches involved (Figure 15.5) showed the center rib lateral cross slots, and the corrugated type sipe pattern was clearly visible. This was not visible in the casting. *Make your own comparison.* With the aid of the tread drawing (Figures 15.6 and 15.7), I then determined that there were three repeating sequences and marked them on the test impression. (Tread drawings are sometimes faded and difficult to read. Fortunately, most of the information in the drawings is not needed by the examiner, but it is for the mold manufacturer.)

I then compared the right rear test impression (Figure 15.8) with the screen positive of the casting (Figure 15.9). In the right rear tire test

**Figure 15.5.** Lateral slots and corrugated sipes visible in test impression of suspect's left rear tire in New Jersey case. *(Courtesy of Charles E. Waldron, New Jersey State Division of Criminal Justice)*

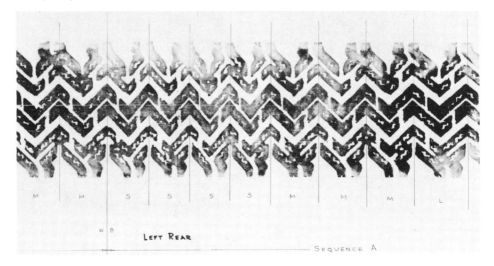

**Figure 15.4.** *(continued)*

impression (sequence A1, Figure 15.10) I looked for *specific* accidental characteristics and found 14, plus one "mold vs. mold" and one general accidental characteristic. Each was identified and numbered on the screen positive (see Figure 15.9) and on the test impression (Figure 15.10). The specific accidental characteristics were also marked with arrows and listed:

1. Notch in shoulder rib Z element, front edge
2. Tapered wear on leading edge of transverse slot
3. Tear at apex of center chevron
4. Notch in shoulder rib Z element, trailing edge
5. A flattened point
6. Distinctive tapered wear on leading edge of transverse slot, plus a flattened point
7. Absence of groove impression at exact location of wear bar (a general accidental characteristic)
8. Bulbous groove opening into trailing edge of center chevron rib element
9. Cut on trailing edge of center chevron rib
10. Cut across point of shoulder Z element
11. Notch in center rib element, front edge
12. Worn configuration of front edge of center element
13. Depression in center rib
14. Misaligned center chevron ("mold vs. mold")

I was therefore able to state that the right rear tire from the suspect's vehicle and the tire that had made the crime scene impression were the same—a positive identification.

The front tires on the suspect's Chevrolet Impala were P235/78R15 B.F. Goodrich Lifesaver XLM steel-belted radials (Figure 15.11) I then compared the front tire test impressions and a muddy imprint depos-

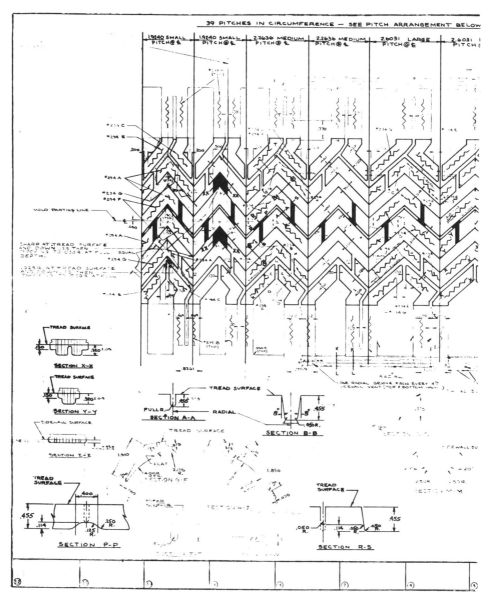

**Figure 15.6.** Tread drawing of Seiberling Snow Power Radial in New Jersey case. *(Courtesy of Firestone Tire & Rubber Co.)*

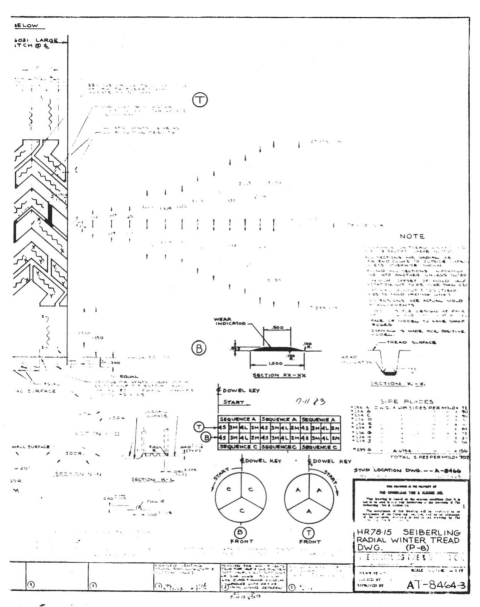

**Figure 15.7.** Tread drawing of Seiberling Snow Power Radial in New Jersey case, with important sections highlighted. *(Courtesy of Firestone Tire & Rubber Co.)*

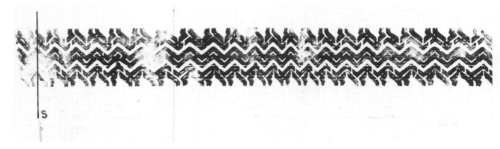

**Figure 15.8.**  Full circumference test impression of suspect's right rear tire in New Jersey case. *(Courtesy of Charles E. Waldron, New Jersey State Division of Criminal Justice)*

ited on the edge of the road at the crime scene (Figure 15.12). The ruler inch marks were not clear, but fortunately the total length was well defined. The following consistencies in the suspect's tires and the crime scene imprint were noted:

1. Both are seven-rib designs.

**Figure 15.9.**  Casting screen positive of suspect's right rear tire in New Jersey case. *(Courtesy of Charles E. Waldron, New Jersey State Division of Criminal Justice)*

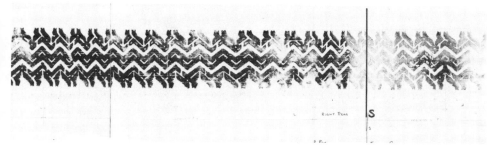

**Figure 15.8.** *(continued)*

2. Both have a center rib that is more narrow than adjacent ribs.
3. Both have a continuous shoulder rib.

Even though the imperfect mud imprint provided little detail, it was significant that that size front tire was on the suspect's Impala. It should be noted that according to the Tire and Rim Association Year Book the largest optional-size tire for an Impala is a H78-15 (see Figure 15.13). The actual size of tire on the Impala was a P235/78R15, which

**Figure 15.10** Test impression of suspect's right rear tire, in New Jersey case, sequence Al showing specific accidental characteristics. *(Courtesy of Charles E. Waldron, New Jersey State Division of Criminal Justice)*

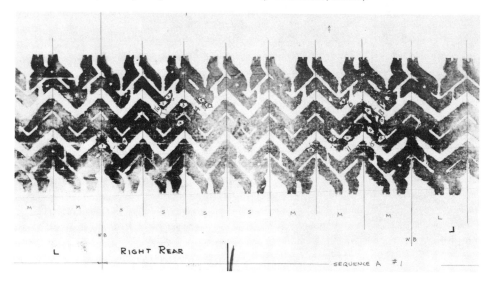

**Figure 15.11.** B.F. Goodrich Lifesaver XLM. *(Courtesy of Charles E. Waldron, New Jersey State Division of Criminal Justice)*

is interchangeable with an L78-15. Notice that the larger size is specified for a Cadillac, which fact alone made this tire size extremely rare and certainly not recommended on a Chevrolet Impala.

In preparation for the trial to follow, Prosecuting Attorney Charles Waldron met with me to gain a complete understanding of my report. He later prepared a summary report that became an excellent outline for my testimony. Before my testimony, a copy of the report submitted by the defendant's expert witness was given to me. One statement in the report read: "Although the receiving soil surface and the plaster cast are not ideal surfaces for comparison of individual detailed

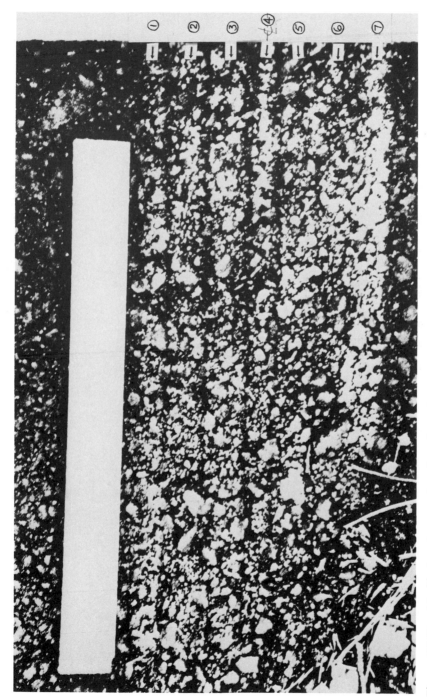

**Figure 15.12.** Muddy imprint on edge of road at crime scene in New Jersey case. *(Courtesy of Charles E. Waldron, New Jersey State Division of Criminal Justice)*

**160**

| CAR MAKE AND MODEL | TIRE | | Rim |
|---|---|---|---|
| | Standard Size † Load Range | Optional Size † Load Range | |

**FORD MOTOR COMPANY (Continued)**

**Montego**

| CAR MAKE AND MODEL | Standard | Optional | Rim |
|---|---|---|---|
| All 250 and 302 Sedan and Hardtop Montego | E78-14/B | F78-14/B | 5-JJ |
| | | F70-14/B | 7-JJ |
| | | G78-14/B | 5-JJ |
| All 351 Montego 250, 302, and 351 Montego MX | F78-14/B | G78-14/B | 5-JJ |
| and Brougham, except | | G70-14/B | 7-JJ |
| 429 | G78-14/B | G70-14/B | 7-JJ |
| All Cyclones, Spoilers, and Boss, except | G70-14/B | G78-14/B | 7-JJ |
| 351 GT | F70-14/B | G78-14/B | 7-JJ |
| All S. W. | G78-14/B | | 5-JJ |

**GENERAL MOTORS CORPORATION**

**Buick**

| CAR MAKE AND MODEL | Standard | Optional | Rim |
|---|---|---|---|
| All Special, except | G78-14/B | H78-14/B | 6-JJ |
| GS (Skylark) 350 | G78-14/B | H78-14/B | 6-JJ |
| | | G70-14/B | 6-JJ |
| GS (Skylark) 400 | G78-14/B | H78-14/B | 6-JJ |
| | | G60-15/B | 7-JJ |
| Sportwagon | H78-14/B | | 6-JJ |
| **LeSabre, Wildcat** | H78-15/B | J78-15/B | 6-JJ |
| **Riviera** except | H78-15/B | | 6-JJ |
| GS | H78-15/B | H70-15/B | 6-JJ |
| **Electra** | J78-15/B | | 6-JJ |
| **Estate Wagon** | L78-15/B | | 6-JJ |

**✱ Cadillac**

| CAR MAKE AND MODEL | Standard | Optional | Rim |
|---|---|---|---|
| All, except | L78-15/B | | 6-JK |
| Eldorado | L78-15/B | | 6-JK |
| Fleetwood 75 | L78-15/D | 8.20-15/D | 6-JK |
| Commercial | 8.90-15/D | | 6-JK |

**✱ Chevrolet**

| CAR MAKE AND MODEL | Standard | Optional | Rim |
|---|---|---|---|
| All 6-Cyl. Sedan, H. T., Convertible, | F78-15/B | | 5-JJ |
| Biscayne & Bel-Air with base 350 V-8 | or G78-15/B | | 5-JJ |
| | | G78-15/B | 6-JK |
| | | H78-15/B | 6-JK |
| | | G70-15/B | 6-JK |
| All Other Biscayne, Bel-Air, Impala | G78-15/B | | 5-JJ |
| and Caprice except | | H78-15/B | 6-JK |
| | | G70-15/B | 6-JK |
| 454 | H78-15/B | H70-15/B | 6-JK |
| Station Wagons | H78-15/D | | 6-JK |

**Monte Carlo**

| CAR MAKE AND MODEL | Standard | Optional | Rim |
|---|---|---|---|
| All, except | G78-15/B | | 6-JK |
| | | G70-15/B | 7-JJ |
| 454 | G70-15/B | | 7-JJ |

**Nova**

| CAR MAKE AND MODEL | Standard | Optional | Rim |
|---|---|---|---|
| All, except | E78-14/B | | 5-JJ |
| | | E70-14/B | 6-JK |
| SS | E70-14/B | | 7-JJ |

**Figure 15.13.** Cadillac and Chevrolet size tires compared. *(Courtesy of Tire and Rim Association)*

impressions, the color photographs and the plaster cast did exhibit sufficient class characteristics to demonstrate that this impression was made by the same type of tire as HR78-15 Seiberling Radial Winter Tread Tire." My concerns were about the incomplete aspects of the report:

1. An expert should be specific about which Seiberling tire design he or she is referring to, not just say "Seiberling Radial Winter Tread Tire." There are four similar Seiberling snow tires (see Figure 15.3), but *notice the differences.*
2. Many other designs have similar tread patterns, but the report from this casual examination states that there were "sufficient class characteristics to demonstrate that this impression was made by the same type of HR78-15 Seiberling Radial Winter Tread Tire." But no tire of that design name exists.
3. There is no reference to an examination for general or specific accidental characteristics.

If tire specialists followed certain basic procedures, there would be more consistency. The absence of a thorough examination can be misleading and undermines expert testimony. In this specific case, Judge Reginald Staton suggested that standards for examining tire imprints are needed. I hope that the standards and procedures set forth in Chapter 9 (esp. Table 9.1) meet that challenge. The jury found James Koedatich guilty.

# Traffic Accident Investigation

# 16

*A motor vehicle is used in 75 percent of all the major crimes reported today. Damage to the vehicle at the crime scene may leave vehicle-related evidence, such as headlight fragments, paint chips, or oil drippings, which the criminal investigator can recover and examine to identify the vehicle. But often the only evidence remaining at the scene of a crime is a tire imprint.*

(Given, Nehrich, and Shields 1977)

Investigators should be alert for valuable tire imprint evidence that may be at the scene of a traffic accident. The same procedures for recording tire imprints at the scene of a crime should be followed when investigating traffic accidents.

In a traffic accident the investigator often has an advantage over the general crime scene investigator when looking for tire impressions. It can be assumed that the area to be investigated is generally well defined.

Tire imprints may be visible in a traffic accident dependent on many factors: snow covered roads, wet or dry dusty conditions, soft or hard pavement, smooth or sticky surfaces, or even if the tire has carried a foreign substance to the scene. If objects are involved, they should be properly photographed or lifted at the location and then recovered.

If tire tracks are not visible but suspected in a specific area, protect that area until dark, then try viewing the surface with a flashlight directed from a low angle across the surface being searched. If imprints are located, they should be photographed or lifted. (Recall the latent imprint recovery methods described by Lawren Nause and Stephen Ojena in Chapter 6.)

## Skid and Scuff Marks

If properly recorded, skid marks can sort out basically different tread designs—for example, a five-rib design leaves an imprint different from that of a three-rib tire design. The relationship of rib widths may also be determined. There are two types of skid marks: acceleration marks and deceleration marks.

### Acceleration Marks

If the drive tires are spinning faster than the vehicle speed, heavy burn marks will be left on the pavement at the initial point of acceleration. This may be called "laying a patch," "laying rubber," or "burning rubber." Tire rib definition may be most obvious in the center of the imprint.

### Deceleration Marks

If a tire rotates much more slowly than the vehicle speed because of braking or downshifting, deceleration marks will be left on the pavement. During heavy braking, a greater portion of the vehicle load is transmitted to the outer edges of the front tires. Parallel shoulder skid marks will be well defined. Wear and inflation are also factors that may modify the appearance of the tread marks.

### Scuff Marks

Little tread identification may be gained from scuff marks. They may indicate only the vehicle's path of travel and the fact that it is out of control.

### Case Study 16.1

In this case, identification of which vehicle made the skid marks was crucial in determining who was responsible for the accident. In 1982 I was asked to help identify tire skid marks left at the scene of a serious traffic accident. The question was: "Which of two possible trucks, if either, made the skid mark?" Unfortunately, none of the many general scene photographs had been taken perpendicular to the highway surface and with a scale.

Both trucks involved in the accident had three-rib tire designs, and such designs are typically very similar (see Figure 16.1). The photographic information I received did not help me determine which tire design had made the skid marks. No scale was shown in the photograph, and the extreme angle of obliquity distorted the

**Figure 16.1.** Three rib truck tire designs can be very similar. *(Courtesy of Firestone Tire & Rubber Co.)*

width of the skid mark. I could not be of service with only poor photographs to examine.

### Case Study 16.2

In an accident case, *Rafael Garcia et al. v. Dodge Motors et al.* (1982), tire identification procedures helped resolve the dispute.

Firestone had supposedly mounted Firestone tires on the vehicle in question prior to the accident, but I was asked to examine scene photographs to determine the tire manufacturer and design. The right front, left front, and left rear tires were in question. Fortunately, I had many good-quality photographs of the overturned vehicle to review.

Examination of Figures 16.2 and 16.3 with magnification showed that two of the three tires were B.F. Goodrich—not Firestone, as charged. One was belted bias, the other was bias-ply construction. In part because it had come to light that the replacement tires were a "mixed bag," a reasonable and intelligent settlement was reached.

It must be remembered that most suspect vehicles leave the scene of a crime going forward, so investigators generally find evidence of rear tire imprints. Also, if a person or object is struck by a vehicle, it may

**Figure 16.2.** Whose tires were on this vehicle? *(Courtesy of Scott R. Stevenson, Hinshaw, Culbertson, Moelmann, Hoban & Fuller, Attorneys-at-Law)*

not be the front tires that leave the imprint, the trailing rear tires, driven over the object last, may be most visible. Rear tire imprints often obliterate the front tire imprints.

Rear tires are not only more often recorded, they also may have more specific accidental characteristics than front tires. Compared with front tires, rear tires suffer a significantly greater amount of punctures due to highway debris. Nails are the most common source of punctures. A nail, bottle, or piece of glass or sharp metal will lie flat on the highway. If a front tire ran over the object, it would be flipped up so that it might be wedged into or strike the trailing rear tire in such a way that the tire would be cut. Worn tires have a considerably higher incidence of punctures than tires with a greater tread depth. Also, flat tires and wet weather are not just a coincidence of bad luck. Water is a good lubricant for rubber, making it much easier for a sharp object to penetrate a tire.

In a hit-and-run accident, the victim should be examined for a tire imprint. The investigator should look at the clothing as well as the victim's body (see Case Study 16.3, below). If more than one tire

**Figure 16.3.** Whose tires were on this vehicle? *(Courtesy of Scott R. Stevenson, Hinshaw, Culbertson, Moelmann, Hoban & Fuller, Attorneys-at-Law)*

imprint can be found, even general accidental characteristics can develop strong probability evidence.

### Case Study 16.3

In the case of *William Lyons et al. v. Big Springs (Texas) Herald et al.* (1985), a little girl named Vickie was run over by a vehicle. Vickie's mother was working at the *Big Springs Herald* newspaper while her daughter played in the parking lot. No one witnessed which vehicle had driven over Vickie, and the lot was so bumpy that the driver might well not have known he had hit her.

Vickie's mother suspected three vehicles. Later, on her own initiative, Vickie's mother took what we would call test impressions of the tires on those vehicles. She wiped shoepolish on a portion of the tires from each of the suspect vehicles, laid typing paper on that area of each tire, and with a comb took a rubbing of a portion of each tire tread and then recorded on each rubbing the vehicle name and tire position. Three years after the accident, an

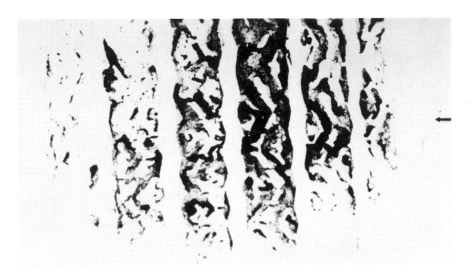

**Figure 16.4.** Right front tire shoepolish test impression. *(Courtesy of Roy E. Brown, Brown Todd, Hagood & Davenport, Attorneys-at-Law)*

attorney asked me to help determine which of the three vehicles, if any, had driven over Vickie.

The tire tread patterns on two of the vehicles were clearly different from the impression on Vicki's forehead. (Vickie is alive but will be in need of considerable care for the rest of her life.) I was furnished with all the shoepolish test impressions. The right front tire imprint from a newspaper truck is shown in Figure 16.4. I also had been given a color photograph taken at the hospital after the accident (Figure 16.5), clearly showing a tire imprint on Vickie's forehead. The blood had risen to the surface in the exact location of the grooves, and even the narrow sipes were well defined. Unfortunately no ruler was included for scale.

I asked that a new photograph of Vickie's face be taken at the same angle and with a ruler included. Then the original hospital photograph was overlayed with the new 1 : 1 photograph to determine a more accurate enlargement to be compared with the tire test impression.

The next step was to identify the shoepolish test impressions from the three vehicles. Checking each against the impression on Vickie's forehead, two of the vehicles were quickly eliminated. The third vehicle was a newspaper delivery truck that had tire tread patterns that looked much like the imprint on Vickie's forehead.

I was also provided with a Golden Sonic 78 tire manufactured by

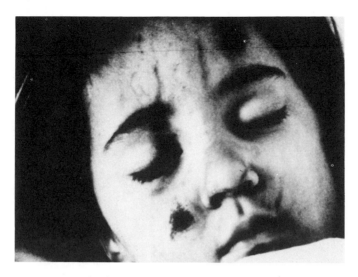

**Figure 16.5.** Hospital photograph of Vickie's face. *(Courtesy of Roy E. Brown, Brown, Todd, Hagood & Davenport, Attorneys-at-Law)*

Kelly-Springfield. This tire was the same design and size as shown in the rubbings taken from the newspaper's Ford pickup truck. Sales slips recovered from the tire distributor showed that these tires had been sold to the newspaper for the pickup truck. Three years later, the truck was not available, but the records were.

I also obtained tread drawings of the Golden Sonic 78 tire to thoroughly acquaint myself with the tread details. The tire was mounted on a Ford pickup and a full-circumference inked test impression was made. The tread drawing made it possible for me to define the pitch sequence.

After studying the original photograph of Vickie (Figure 16.5), now to scale, it was apparent which of two rib widths had made the impression on Vickie's forehead. The worn sipe pattern of these two ribs, shown in the test impression, helped eliminate three of the four Sonic tires on the pickup truck. It was now clear that the right front tire, with its exposed sipe tie bars, could have made the imprint. Careful attention to the right front tire made it possible to determine that the pitches defined on Vickie's forehead were the number 10 pitch lengths, clearly not 8 or 12. An overlay (Figure 16.6) dramatized the correlation (this was more apparent in color).

It was not possible to make a positive identification because there were no visible specific accidental characteristics and I did not have the actual right front tire, only a short shoepolish test

**Figure 16.6.** Overlay of right front tire shoepolish test impression on Vickie's face showing consistent accidental characteristics.

impression. But there were enough general accidental characteristics to convince the owners of the pickup truck that they had been responsible.

Photography was the best method of recording the very fragile evidence on Vickie's forehead. Fortunately, the impressions healed and are no longer visible.

# Future Trends and Considerations

**17**

*Tire technology is anticipating future transportation demands. Needed tire innovation efforts can be categorized by analyzing the functional aspects of the tire. These functional areas are performance (how it works), reliability (eliminate spare tire), and ecology (how it affects society).*

(Kovac 1978)

The tire is an ever-changing, complex component of a vehicle. It is important to be alert to the technological developments in tire manufacturing and design. New tread designs are constantly being developed, modified, and even copied by the competition.

## Segmented Molds

Some major tire manufacturers are molding tires with segmented molds, as opposed to the more conventional full-circle or "clamshell molds." Segmented molds do not separate in the center area of the tread, but they do separate in short lateral sections (see Figure 17.1). Segmented molds produce more precise tires and allow for more aggressive, deep tread patterns with harder tread compounds. Regardless of the additional mold costs, this segmented process is expected to continue. The sequence of pitches in segmented molds is often difficult to analyze, so it is increasingly important for the examiner to have tread drawings for reference.

## Original Equipment Tires

To lower costs for the supplier, some vehicle manufacturers are purchasing one tire brand from Company A in only a few sizes for

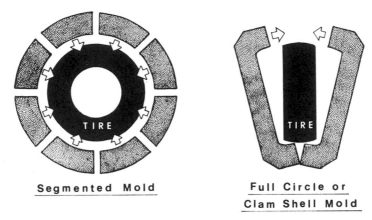

**Segmented Mold**          **Full Circle or Clam Shell Mold**

**Figure 17.1.** Schematic of a segmented mold operation vs. a full circle or clam shell mold.

specific vehicles, and another tire brand from Company B in different sizes for certain other vehicles. This information could be useful to the examiner. If a tire is identified as original equipment, this could narrow a search down to a relatively few vehicle models. The tire manufacturer's sales department may be able to identify the types of vehicles normally using a certain size and design.

## Front-Wheel Drive

With the increased use of front-wheel-drive vehicles and the generally accepted practice of leaving all-season tires on year-round, snow tire sales are gradually diminishing. Studded snow tire sales already diminished greatly, partly because of limitations on which months of the year they may be legally used. All-season designs now have a greater share of the market.

## Four-Wheel Steering

A University of Michigan survey reported that four-wheel steering has great potential for growth in the passenger car market. As of this writing, Mazda Motor Corporation and Honda Motor Company have introduced four-wheel steering in the United States (Figure 17.2). This will affect the information gained from recording turning diameter measurements if all tires are turning.

Four-wheel steer (4WS) systems are designed to enhance vehicle stability and to improve maneuverability and handling, particularly when cornering or changing lanes at high speeds. New tires and tread patterns may evolve for the 4WS system.

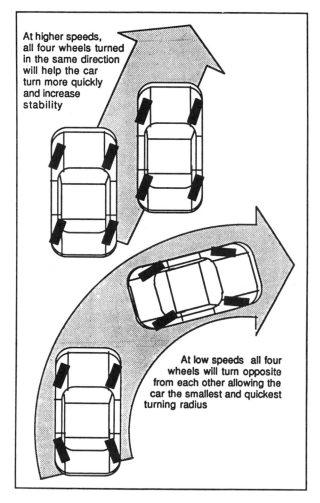

At higher speeds, all four wheels turned in the same direction will help the car turn more quickly and increase stability

At low speeds all four wheels will turn opposite from each other allowing the car the smallest and quickest turning radius

**Figure 17.2.** Four-wheel steering vehicles will leave different tire tracks than front wheel steering vehicles. *(Courtesy of the* Cleveland Plain Dealer*)*

## Spare Tires

Years ago the spare tire in the trunk was simply an extra, identical to the four tires on the new vehicle. Around 1975, as Detroit auto manufacturers tried to improve gasoline economy by shaving every possible ounce of weight from their vehicles, a new lightweight spare emerged. These compact spares weigh 10 to 15 pounds less than full-size tires but still meet safety and strength requirements. According to studies at General Motors, spare tires are generally used for no more than 20 to 30 miles before the flat is repaired or replaced. It is unlikely that a criminal would leave the scene of a crime with this type of spare, although criminals can have bad days too.

Compact spares are not listed in the *Tread Design Guide*. Original equipment tire manufacturers are the prime suppliers of compact spares. Some of these spares have lettering in the tread. They are generally narrow and have little or no noise treatment. Uniroyal Goodrich Tire Company has announced an airless polyurethane mini-spare. Other manufacturers are developing similar concepts.

## Bladders

Tires are formed from the inside with an inflated rubber bladder. Bladders are designed with channels and patterns to vent air at the inside surface of the tire. Manufacturers have different systems and patterns for accomplishing venting, so if an investigator has only the inside of a tire to examine, the manufacturer may still be identified. In tire identification, this might be at least collateral evidence.

I was once shown an innertube that had the bladder pattern clearly transferred from the inner surface of a tire. A section of the innertube was used as a handgun silencer—the manufacturer of the tire on which the innertube was installed was identified.

## Retreads

It is important to distinguish between retreading and recapping. *Retreading* is "the process of renewing the tread on a tire by buffing the old surface and applying a new tread. It differs from recapping in that new rubber is applied to both the tread surface and shoulder area of the tire." *Recapping* is "in general terms, same as retreading. More specifically, it refers to the process known as 'top-capping,' in which pre-cured rubber is applied to only the tread surface of the tire" (Rubber Manufacturers Association 1981).

A worn-out tire tread may have a casing that will continue to give satisfactory service if fitted with another tread. Retreads can be perfectly safe if properly prepared. Commercial aircraft tires are frequently retreaded five or more times. Truck tires may also be retreaded many times, so that more than 200,000 miles of service might be obtained from the same casing.

Occasionally, major manufacturers will produce a retread design that has the same basic tread pattern as a popular new tire in its line. Examiners should be alert to the lack of a parting line location and a generally less complex noise treatment in retreads. If a portion of the sidewall impression is visible, it may be obvious that the tire is a retread.

Retreads of one design may be found on a casing of another manufacturer. The *Tread Design Guide* has a section on both truck and passenger car retreads. Always check that section when determining tread designs.

Recapped tires may have a lateral visible splice (joint) in one location around the circumference. These tread designs generally have very simple repeating pitch sequences. Retreading and recapping may be difficult to recognize. If an investigator wishes to understand more about retread tires, Bennett Garfield has prepared a book *Who Retreads Tires*. The book describes how to read identification numbers and lists retread plant code marks and matrix manufacturer name and address information.

## Changing Tread Designs

Significant new tread identification features are constantly developing. The investigator must be aware of new possibilities all the time. In every tire identification case in which I have been involved, new features and new tread identification considerations have come to my attention to broaden my experience and expertise.

Progress in tire design is made in steps; there are few quantum leaps. Tire manufacturers that supply the auto industry are continually being pressed to make small improvements. Investigators of tire imprints should keep up-to-date by asking questions of those experienced in the field and maintain yearly tread design guides.

Fortunately for tire investigation, we live in a competitive economy, with thousands of different tread designs. If there is a consumer need, some designer will develop a tire to satisfy that need. This constant change makes the study of tire imprints continuously challenging. We live in an ever-changing world. There is no "one best design."

# Preparation for Trial  18

*The role of the expert witness is not to determine guilt or innocence, but rather to assist the court in determining what weight is to be placed on technical evidence entered which without assistance could not be interpreted properly.*

(Cassidy 1980)

Tire imprint identification specialists are often called on to testify in court as expert witnesses. The role of the "tire expert" in trial proceedings is threefold:

1. To explain the procedure for examining tire evidence.
2. To give an authoritative opinion on the evidence relating to tire imprints.
3. To emphasize the importance of the case merely by his or her presence.

## What Is an Expert Witness?

The court quite properly determines who is an "expert." The court weighs the qualifications, experience, and demeanor of a tire imprint specialist carefully every time the specialist appears. In addition, the individual examiner's experience and attention to detail will help determine the value that the court or jury places on the evidence.

The expert witness is allowed to give an opinion on any relevant issue that is within the scope of his or her expertise. All other witnesses must testify only as to facts within their personal knowledge. The expert witness is not required to have been at the scene. The tire expert is presumed to be an impartial, disinterested person who is simply explaining things (a significant reason for employing the services of an unbiased consultant).

## What Is a Tire Imprint Identification Expert?

A Tire imprint identification expert must be knowledgeable in many areas:

1. Methods of photographing tire imprints
2. Methods of preparing prints and screen positives
3. Methods of recording imprints
4. Reading tire mold drawings
5. Tire construction and nomenclature
6. Tread patterns and sources of reference
7. Tire mold and design features
8. Methods of recording test impressions
9. Methods of determining pitch sequence
10. Standards for tire imprint identification

In order to present tire footprint identification evidence in court, an expert must also have training and experience in the field. Tire identification training is available, and experience in similar investigative work can be acquired before giving testimony in a case requiring tire identification. The Tire Imprint Identification Checklist (Table 9.1) identifies the major features of tire imprints that an expert must review.

## The Tire Expert's Testimony

If a thorough written report was prepared, the examiner can describe the steps of the investigation chronologically. Remember, the investigator's notes and report are subject to subpoena during a trial, so it is advisable that they be legible and clear in case they will be read and interpreted at a later date.

Tire imprint identification experts can promote better understanding with the court and help their audiences discriminate between true scientific evidence and pseudo-scientific claims if they translate their ideas and professional jargon into lay terms. This may take longer, but it will clarify the final conclusion. Do not arrive at a conclusion too quickly. Attorneys find that a precise, visual correlation of tire impressions with the tire that made them is an invaluable tool that a judge and jury can clearly understand.

When testifying, tire experts may give their opinions on a number of aspects:

1. They may speak to the specific accidental characteristics. For example, the crime scene tire imprint is identified as having been made by the tire in question; only the tire in question could have made the crime scene impression—a positive identification.
2. They may speak to general accidental characteristics. For example, the chances of another tire having all the same class characteristics and general accidental characteristics is highly unlikely.
3. They may speak to class characteristics. For example, the crime scene tire impression is consistent with the imprint made by the suspect's tire or any other tire of the same tread design and size, or the crime scene tire impression is *not* consistent with the imprint made by the suspect's tire in question.

## Courtroom Evidence Displays

Each tire identification case will be handled with different evidence, data, and visual aids. Because tire treads are significantly more complicated to explain than shoe, foot, or finger prints, a technique of identification that requires educating the jury is necessary. The following items are meant to be only a guide to possible educational and evidence displays that may be used in court:

1. Full-size photographs of the crime scene imprint. These should have pertinent pitch lengths and accidental characteristics clearly defined. Mount photographs on rigid foamcore boards for easy handling and display.
2. Full-size screen positives made from the crime scene imprints.
3. Castings, if available.
4. Test impressions of all tires on the vehicle in question. These boards may be as large as 1' × 9'. Consider how this will be physically displayed in the courtroom prior to testifying. Test impressions should have pertinent pitch lengths and characteristics clearly defined.
5. The actual mounted tire or tires should be on display with pertinent pitch lengths and characteristics clearly defined. For better viewing, elevate the tire vertically on a table in a stand (Figure 18.1).
6. A general scene photograph and/or sketch.
7. An enlarged Tire Imprint Identification Checklist makes a good visual display of features to be reviewed in testimony.
8. Projected slides or photo enlargements of crime scene imprint vs. test impression side-by-side to enhance understanding of the evidence.

**Figure 18.1.** Tire display showing area identified with contrasting arrows.

9. An easel pad of paper and a large pen to help describe tire features. This is preferable to a chalkboard, because drawings may become court evidence.

## Typical Questions in Cross-Examination

Potential cross-examination questions should be discussed prior to trial with the attorney. Some of the more common questions should be answered in the initial testimony (the best defense is often a good offense). A tire expert can expect certain basic questions in cross-examination. These always seem to come up in some form and should be considered.

Q: How many tires of this specific design are in existence?

Initially this sounds like a very good question, because thousands of tire designs are produced yearly. If a positive identification is sought, it might seem like finding a needle in a haystack, but if that question is broken down it will be more meaningful and less awesome.

As preparation for this type of question, first gather some of the following information about the specific design in question from the sales department of the manufacturer:

Number of sizes

Percentage of sales by size

Number of tires of identified size produced

Years in production (or is it still being produced)

Number of molds of the identified size

Projected life-span of the tire in years

How the tread design may have changed

The percentage of sales of black sidewalls, white stripe, or white letters

The number of tires sold in the geographical area

Whether the design is made primarily for O.E. sales, trade sales, or private brand sales

After compiling all available and pertinent information, an explanation of the data gathered will answer the above question more accurately.

Q: How many specific accidental characteristics are required to make a positive identification?

A: One.

Then clarify that answer by reviewing the investigation process, pointing out each correlation of a crime-scene imprint with the tire in question:

Brand vs. brand

Mold vs. mold

General accidental characteristics

Specific accidental characteristics

At this point the examiner can focus on a single specific accidental characteristic and progressively describe its location. In order to make a positive identification, use this general format:

One specific passenger or truck tire
One specific design
One specific size
One specific mold
One specific position on the vehicle
One specific pitch length

One specific rib
One specific sequence of pitches
One specific location
One specific tread element
One specific depth
One specific accidental feature

This is only an illustration. Modifications to correspond to the available evidence will be necessary.

An alternate answer to the above question would be:

A: A positive tire imprint identification is established by agreement of class characteristics and accidental characteristics of such significance or number that no other logical conclusion can be reached.

The questioning may continue:

Q: Is tire imprint identification an exact science?

A: It is quite exact. Tires reproduce exactly the features of the mold in which they are vulcanized. Imprints made by tires faithfully reflect the general characteristics of the tire that made the imprint as well as any special accidental characteristics of that tire, such as a cut, and therefore permit a direct correlation, much as the process of determining that a document was produced on a certain typewriter that had a particular damaged letter. Tire imprints are never perfect, but in this case the significant portion of the imprint is clear enough for me to be quite sure of the opinion I have given.

Q: How can you compare a recently prepared test tire impression with a crime scene imprint that may have developed worn variations over hundreds or even thousands of miles of use?

A: Obviously, it would be better to have limited wear from the time the crime scene imprint was recorded to the time of the test imprint. However, many specific accidental characteristics will be retained. New characteristics that may be added with wear will not necessarily affect the analysis.

It is good to remember that if the tread of a new passenger tire is 0.40" deep and wears at approximately 0.01" per thousand miles until worn out at 40,000 miles, that is clearly very slow wear. Therefore, a few months of wear or a few thousand miles may not noticeably change the general accidental characteristics. Typically, the rate of wear diminishes over the life of the tire.

Q: How can you compare a soft-surface or varied-substance imprint with a hard cardboard test impression?

A: A light-colored hard-cardboard surface and a contrasting black-ink test impression clearly illustrate tire element characteristics. Not all test impression characteristics will be as visible in the less perfect crime scene imprint. However, specific accidental characteristics are of such size and geometric shape in one specific location that they positively correlate with another less precise configuration. Trying to duplicate the crime scene surface is unreliable and actually a hindrance.

Q: If it is difficult to measure the tread width (arc width) accurately, how can you confirm the tire size from a crime scene photograph?

A: Measurements taken laterally between widespread points in the crime scene imprint compare dimensionally with the same relative points on the test impression.

Q: How can you compare a test impression with a crime scene tire imprint made by a vehicle with unknown load and a tire with unknown air pressure?

A: It is primarily tread elements that are examined. Vehicle weight and tire air pressure may affect the groove opening or closing, but the tread elements remain relatively unchanged.

Q: If there are no established standards for this relatively new field of tire imprint identification, how can you testify as an expert?

A: The standards, theory, and techniques used in tire imprint identification are not entirely new, nor are they a revolutionary approach to examining evidence. My extensive experience in [tire design, fingerprinting, photography, footwear identification, handwriting comparisons, or whatever is applicable] provides a solid background for my ability to relate tire imprints to the tire that made them.

*Note:* The comparison of crime scene castings or photographs with test impressions of a suspect's vehicle is very dramatic. When interviewing or interrogating a suspect, prior to trial this compelling visual evidence may help elicit a confession and save a lot of valuable time and energy.

# Obtaining a Consultant 19

*One cannot expect a quality investigation if the technical consultant is given inadequate time for preparation and analysis.*
(Genck 1987)

A tire imprint identification consultant can sometimes be of assistance in certain court cases. This chapter looks at the procedures used by such a consultant and at the materials a consultant will need.

## What a Consultant Does

Tire imprint specialists provide four basic types of services:

1. They *study* crime scene imprints, research possible tire designs, prepare test impressions, and analyze and evaluate the findings.
2. They *evaluate* the merits of a potential claim and document their work with an oral and/or written report of their findings. They give an opinion about the merits of the claim.
3. They make *recommendations* concerning certain aspects of litigation procedure (for example, the client or attorney may not be accusing the right party). The consultant may know the opposing specialist and can project the arguments he or she may use. Such recommendations make specialists valuable assistants to the client or attorney.
4. They *testify* in depositions and in court to explain and then defend the technical conclusions they have reached.

A consultant can generally be of help whether there is a suspect or not. If no suspect exists, tire imprints and measurements are recorded. Ask the consultant for a report describing possible tire design or designs, size, manufacturer; a possible vehicle description; and any additional information that may be derived from the evidence provided. If there is a suspect's vehicle, test tire impressions and measurements of the suspect's tires are made and recorded. Ask the consultant for a report describing the procedure followed and the conclusions arrived at in determining the consistency of crime scene imprints vs. suspect's tire test impressions.

## Hiring a Consultant

The tire consultant is generally contacted verbally and should be provided with a clear description of the available evidence. This will allow the prospective consultant to determine whether he or she will be able to help. Fees, anticipated expenses, and estimated costs are usually discussed at this point. The consultant may determine that a retainer is needed before proceeding. The time frame should also be clearly understood. If all parties agree, the consultant should receive a "letter of engagement" to formalize the contract. The consultant should send a letter describing his or her credentials.

At the initial contact with a tire imprint specialist, an attorney might ask for information that cannot be given without a review of the evidence. In a responsible client-attorney relationship, the strengths and weaknesses of a case will be set out as soon as possible. A tire specialist is hired to provide an objective opinion, not just good news.

## Submitting Evidence to a Consultant

When submitting evidence to a consultant, the following information should be prepared:

1. The case number and a brief description of the crime.
2. The general crime scene photograph and/or sketch, indicating imprint locations.
3. Full-size 1 : 1 black-and-white prints of *all* photographed tire imprints or photos of castings (castings may be retained). If unable to prepare 1 : 1 prints, send all negatives.
4. Wheelbase and tire stance measurements (if available).
5. Full-circumference test impressions of all suspect vehicle tires (include spare if applicable). If test impressions cannot be prepared, mounted tires can be bagged and shipped to the consultant. Mark the tire position—RF, LF, RR, LR, and Spare—and furnish vehicle make, model, and year. As an alternative, the consultant may travel to the location of the suspect's vehicle to prepare test impressions and review the above material.

If no suspect exists, only items 1 through 4 will be required.

Necessary screen positives will be prepared by the consultant as required. This may avoid unnecessary and costly screen positives. The tire consultant will need all tire evidence for investigation. This can be achieved by:

1. Postal delivery of the evidence to the consultant.
2. Hand-carrying the evidence to the consultant, which may be necessary, depending on items to be transported. The initial investigator may be the most appropriate person to hand-carry the evidence. If arrangements are made ahead, it may be possible for the courier to stay and look over the shoulder of the consultant as the evidence is examined. This can develop good communications and become a learning experience for the investigator. For the consultant to do the job well, all material must be available.
3. Having the consultant travel to the source of evidence. This will ensure that all evidence is properly prepared. It has the added advantage of training investigators while working with them on the job. Also, if additional information is required, it may be prepared without interruption.

At the end of the investigation, the consultant normally gives a verbal report and follows it with a detailed written report. All material evidence can then be prepared by the consultant for future review and eventual testimony.

All parties should meet prior to the trial. The consultant should thoroughly explain the chronological procedure of investigation and the resultant opinion. Potential cross-examination questions should be considered to avoid surprises.

## A Mission Analysis for Consultants

As a tire imprint identification specialist, I have my own procedures and standards, which tire imprint identification specialists may want to adopt:

*Quality:* Established professional procedures will be followed.

*Cost effectiveness:* A proven effective system will be used to avoid wasted time.

*Timeliness:* Reports and studies will be provided as agreed to.

*Accuracy:* Cross-examination will not weaken the substance of the report.

*Thoroughness:* All items pertinent to the investigation will be reviewed.

*Innovative:* Because each investigation is unique, creative analysis will be made.

# Tire Imprint
# Identification Training 20

*The more technical knowledge a police officer possesses, the greater the probability of securing not only a criminal arrest but also a guilty verdict from the jury.*

(Howell 1988)

I have prepared a two-day seminar/workshop for people interested in examining tire evidence. Those who can learn quite well from written material may find this book sufficient. Others may learn best from hearing the instructions and then having actual hands-on experience with test cases, using this book as a reference for future investigations.

The agenda for the first day of instruction basically encompasses the material presented in this book. Professionally prepared color slides keep the course interesting and informative. Three videotapes augment the training throughout the two-day presentation:

1. *A Tire Factory Tour.* A thorough understanding of the product being investigated is essential. A tour of a tire factory can be invaluable, but this is obtained most practically with an excellent up-to-date 45-minute videotape that explains the history of rubber and current technology in the development and production of automobile tires. The tape also shows computerized tire design methods, tire-testing methods, and various stages of tire production.
2. *An Actual Homicide Case.* Another videotape, prepared by *PM Magazine,* is a reenactment of an actual homicide case I helped solve. The tire impression casting procedure is described, photographs are taken, the design is identified, a suspect is apprehended,

the analysis of the suspect's tires is described, a positive identification is made, and the suspect is convicted—all in 12 minutes of tape.

3. *Preparing an Inked Test Impression.* A third videotape, prepared by the F.B.I. Academy, shows how an inked test impression is prepared. After viewing this tape, each investigator then practices the procedure on a vehicle in the area and analyzes the practice test impressions for noise treatment and accidental characteristics. Identification of specific pitch lengths and determination of the sequence of pitches is attempted without the aid of tread drawings.

On the second day students are furnished the material needed to solve many actual cases. Working out test problems is the best way to learn this very specialized identification procedure. Such test cases encompass all the major points described in the first day of instruction. Students then have an opportunity to present their answers. At the end of the seminar, student evaluations generally report that hands-on experiences were most valuable.

## Test Case Example

The following is an example of one test case and the material provided. Investigators were presented with the following:

1. A crime scene photograph (Figure 20.1). Arrows are normally omitted.
2. A screen positive overlay (Figure 20.2).
3. A 1978 *Tread Design Guide* (Figures 20.3 through 20.9, which represent the significant pages to be reviewed).
4. A 1978 *Who Makes It? and Where? Directory* (Figures 20.10 and 20.11), which represent the significant pages).
5. A portion of the suspect's test impression (Figure 20.12). Arrows are normally omitted.
6. A mold drawing (Figure 20.13). The complete mold drawing is not included because detail is not clear at a reduced scale.

The investigators were asked the following questions. Procedural considerations are given in parentheses after the question if applicable. The answers are also provided.

### Question 1

Using the 1978 *Tread Design Guide*, determine all possible distributors and tire design names that could have made the crime scene imprint. List them. (First one must determine whether the imprint [Figure 20.1] was made by a passenger car tire or a truck tire. The width

**Figure 20.1.** Crime scene tire imprint photograph for workshop test case. (*Courtesy of David S. W. Pong, Riverside County Sheriff, Indio, Calif.*)

**Figure 20.2.** Screen positive overlay made from crime scene tire imprint for workshop test case.

indicates that it was a truck tire. A review of the highway-type truck section of the 1978 *Tread Design Guide* [the appropriate pages are shown in Figures 20.3 through 20.9] turns up the corresponding tread designs. It is important to list *all* possible designs. The center groove is the most characteristic feature to review.)

## Answer

| Distributor | Design |
| --- | --- |
| CBI | Camper Traction (Fig. 20.3) |
| CBI | Big Boss Bruiser (Fig. 20.4) |
| Falcon | Big Boss Bruiser (Fig. 20.5) |
| National | Camper Traction Wide Base (Fig. 20.6) |
| National | XT Commando (Fig. 20.7) |
| Phillips 66 | W/T Trac (Fig. 20.8) |
| Ward | Wide Track LT/RV (Fig. 20.9) |
| Ward | Power Grip Wide Track (Fig. 20.9) |

## Question 2

Determine from the symbols below the photographs in Figures 20.8 and 20.9 which of the above possible designs corresponds exactly to the crime scene photograph and name them. [Figure 20.1 has stud holes highlighted with arrows. The stud hole symbol (SH) is listed for only three designs.]

## Answer

| Distributor | Design |
| --- | --- |
| Phillips 66 | W/T Trac |
| Ward | Wide Track LT/RV |
| Ward | Power Grip Wide Track |

## Question 3

Why are they the only ones?

## Answer

Those designs are the only ones listed that have stud holes.

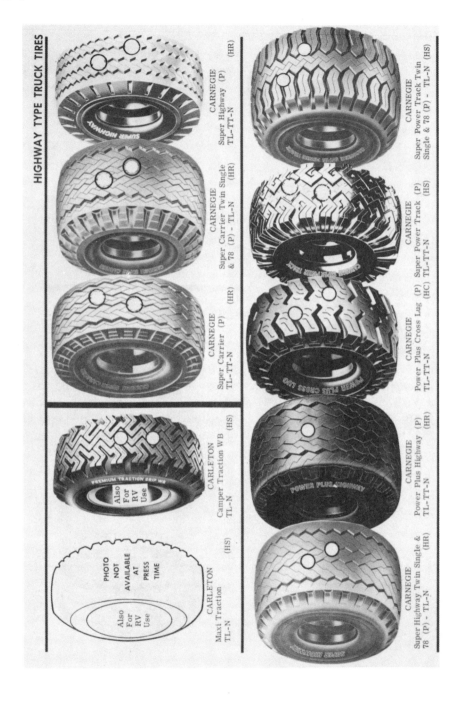

HIGHWAY TYPE TRUCK TIRES

CARNEGIE
Super Highway (P)
TL-TT-N                    (HR)

CARNEGIE
Super Carrier Twin Single
& 78 (P) - TL-N        (HR)

CARNEGIE
Super Carrier (P)
TL-TT-N                    (HR)

CARLETON
Camper Traction WB
TL-N                        (HS)

Also
For
RV
Use

CARLETON
Maxi Traction
TL-N                        (HS)

PHOTO
NOT
AVAILABLE
AT
PRESS
TIME

Also
For
RV
Use

CARNEGIE
Super Power Track Twin
Single & 78 (P) - TL-N  (HS)

CARNEGIE
Super Power Track (P)
TL-TT-N                    (HS)

CARNEGIE
Power Plus Cross Lug (P)
TL-TT-N                    (HC)

CARNEGIE
Power Plus Highway (P)
TL-TT-N                    (HR)

CARNEGIE
Super Highway Twin Single &
78 (P) - TL-N            (HR)

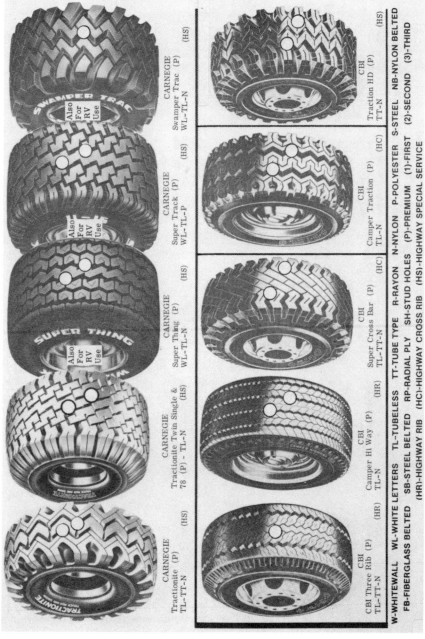

**Figure 20.3.** CBI Camper Traction. *(Courtesy of Al Snyder, editor, Tire Guides Inc.)*

196

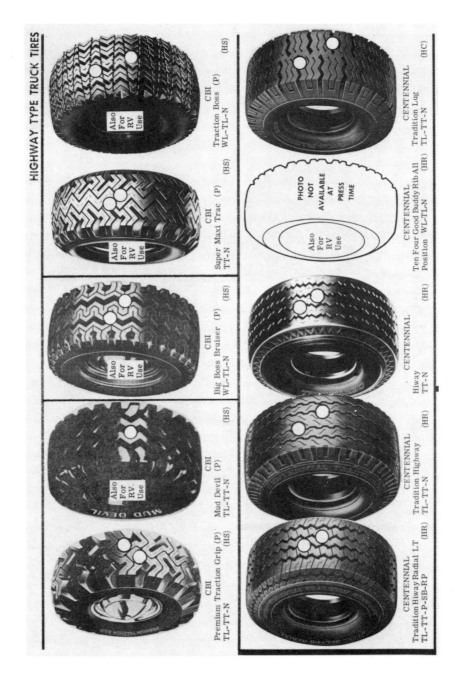

HIGHWAY TYPE TRUCK TIRES

CBI
Traction Boss (P)
WL-TL-N
(HS)

Also
For
RV
Use

CBI
Super Maxi Trac (P)
TT-N
(HS)

Also
For
RV
Use

CBI
Big Boss Bruiser (P)
WL-TL-N
(HS)

Also
For
RV
Use

CBI
Mud Devil (P)
TL-TT-N
(HS)

Also
For
RV.
Use

CBI
Premium Traction Grip (P)
TL-TT-N
(HS)

CENTENNIAL
Tradition Log
TL-TT-N
(HC)

CENTENNIAL
Ten Four Good Buddy Rib All
Position WL-TL-N
(HR)

PHOTO
NOT
AVAILABLE
AT
PRESS
TIME

Also
For
RV
Use

CENTENNIAL
Hiway
TT-N
(HR)

CENTENNIAL
Tradition Highway
TL-TT-N
(HR)

CENTENNIAL
Tradition Hiway Radial LT
TL-TT-P-SB-RP
(HR)

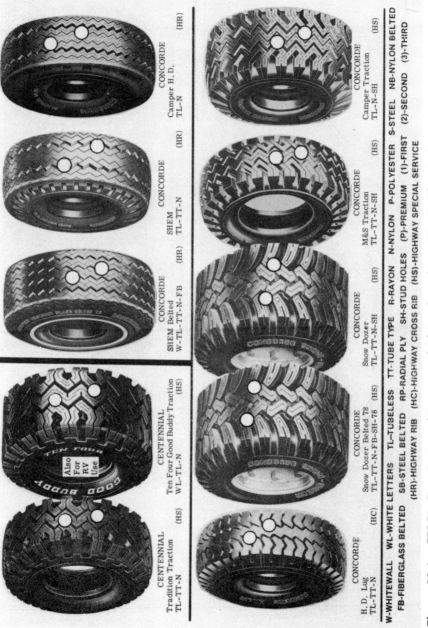

CONCORDE
Camper H. D.
TL-N                                    (HR)

CONCORDE
Camper Traction
TL-N-SH                                 (HS)

CONCORDE
SHEM
TL-TT-N                                 (HR)

CONCORDE
M&S Traction
TL-TT-N-SH                              (HS)

CONCORDE
SHEM Belted
W-TL-TT-N-FB                            (HR)

CONCORDE
Snow Dozer
TL-TT-N-SH                              (HS)

CENTENNIAL
Ten Four Good Buddy Traction
WL-TL-N                                 (HS)

CONCORDE
Snow Dozer Belted 78
TL-TT-N-FB-SH-78                        (HS)

CENTENNIAL
Tradition Traction
TL-TT-N                                 (HS)

H.D. CONCORDE
Lug
TL-TT-N                                 (HC)

W-WHITEWALL   WL-WHITE LETTERS   TL-TUBELESS   TT-TUBE TYPE   R-RAYON   N-NYLON   P-POLYESTER   S-STEEL   NB-NYLON BELTED
FB-FIBERGLASS BELTED   SB-STEEL BELTED   RP-RADIAL PLY   SH-STUD HOLES   (P)-PREMIUM   (1)-FIRST   (2)-SECOND   (3)-THIRD
(HR)-HIGHWAY RIB   (HC)-HIGHWAY CROSS RIB   (HS)-HIGHWAY SPECIAL SERVICE

**Figure 20.4.** CBI Big Boss Bruiser. (*Courtesy of Al Snyder, editor, Tire Guides Inc.*)

198

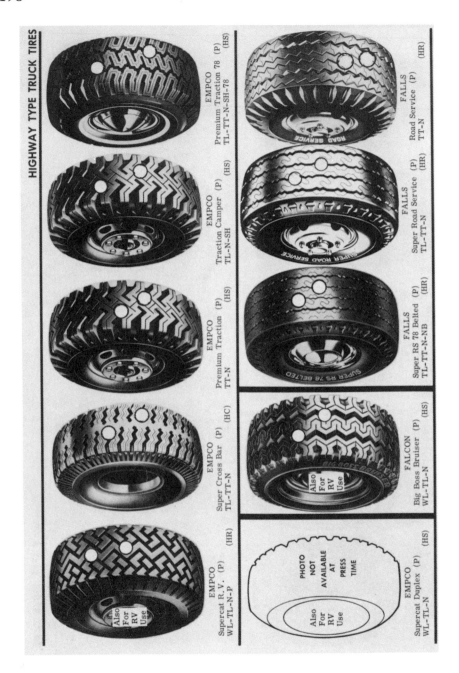

HIGHWAY TYPE TRUCK TIRES

EMPCO
Premium Traction 78 (P)
TL-TT-N-SH-78 (HS)

FALLS
Road Service (P)
TT-N (HR)

EMPCO
Traction Camper (P)
TL-N-SH (HS)

FALLS
Super Road Service (P)
TL-TT-N (HR)

EMPCO
Premium Traction (P)
TT-N (HS)

FALLS
Super RS 78 Belted (P)
TL-TT-N-NB (HR)

EMPCO
Super Cross Bar (P)
TL-TT-N (HC)

FALCON
Big Boss Bruiser (P)
WL-TL-N (HS)
Also For RV Use

EMPCO
Supercat R.V. (P)
WL-TL-N-P (HR)
Also For RV Use

EMPCO
Supercat Duplex (P)
WL-TL-N (HS)
PHOTO NOT AVAILABLE AT PRESS TIME
Also For RV Use

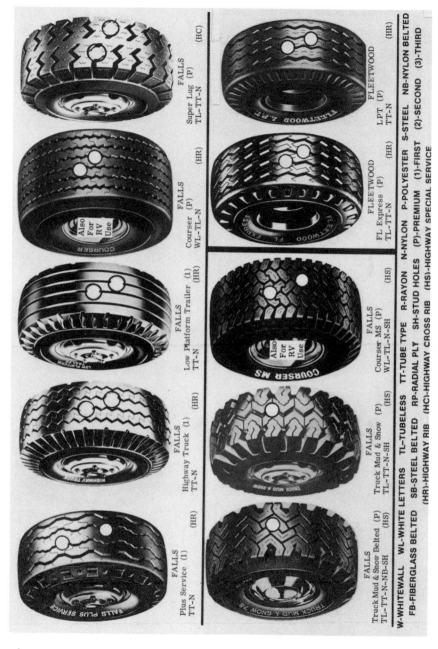

**Figure 20.5.** Falcon Big Boss Bruiser. *(Courtesy of Al Snyder, editor, Tire Guides Inc.)*

FALLS
Plus Service (1)
TT-N
(HR)

FALLS
Highway Truck (1)
TT-N
(HR)

FALLS
Low Platform Trailer (1)
TT-N
(HR)

FALLS
Courser (P)
WL-TL-N
(HR)

FALLS
Super Lug (P)
TL-TT-N
(HC)

FALLS
Truck Mud & Snow Belted (P)
TL-TT-N-NB-SH
(HS)

FALLS
Truck Mud & Snow (P)
TL-TT-N-SH
(HS)

FALLS
Courser MS (P)
WL-TL-N-SH
(HS)

FLEETWOOD
FL Express (P)
TL-TT-N
(HR)

FLEETWOOD
LPT (P)
TT-N
(HR)

W-WHITEWALL   WL-WHITE LETTERS   TL-TUBELESS   TT-TUBE TYPE   R-RAYON   N-NYLON   P-POLYESTER   S-STEEL   NB-NYLON BELTED
FB-FIBERGLASS BELTED   SB-STEEL BELTED   RP-RADIAL PLY   SH-STUD HOLES   (P)-PREMIUM   (1)-FIRST   (2)-SECOND   (3)-THIRD
(HR)-HIGHWAY RIB   (HC)-HIGHWAY CROSS RIB   (HS)-HIGHWAY SPECIAL SERVICE

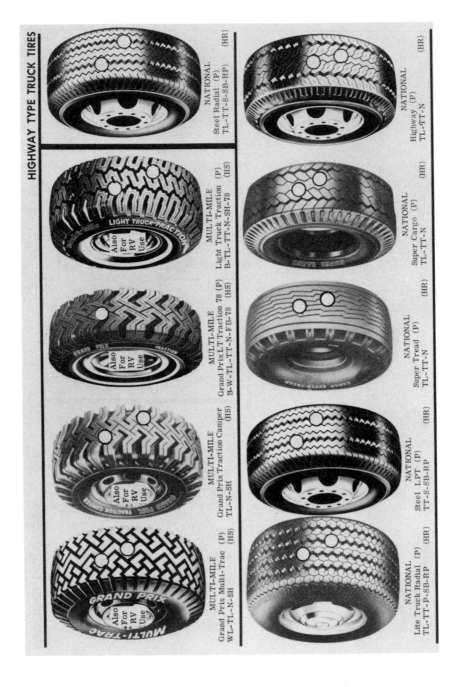

HIGHWAY TYPE TRUCK TIRES

NATIONAL
Steel Radial (P)
TL-TT-S-SB-RP        (HR)

NATIONAL
Highway (P)
TL-TT-N        (HR)

MULTI-MILE
Light Truck Traction (P)        (HS)
B-TL-TT-N-SH-78

NATIONAL
Super Cargo (P)
TL-TT-N        (HR)

MULTI-MILE
Grand Prix LT Traction 78 (P)        (HS)
B-W-TL-TT-N-FB-78

NATIONAL
Super Tread (P)
TL-TT-N        (HR)

MULTI-MILE
Grand Prix Traction Camper        (HS)
TL-N-SH

NATIONAL
Steel LPT (P)
TT-S-SB-RP        (HR)

MULTI-MILE        (P)
Grand Prix Multi-Trac        (HS)
WL-TL-N-SH

NATIONAL
Lite Truck Radial (P)
TL-TT-P-SB-RP        (HR)

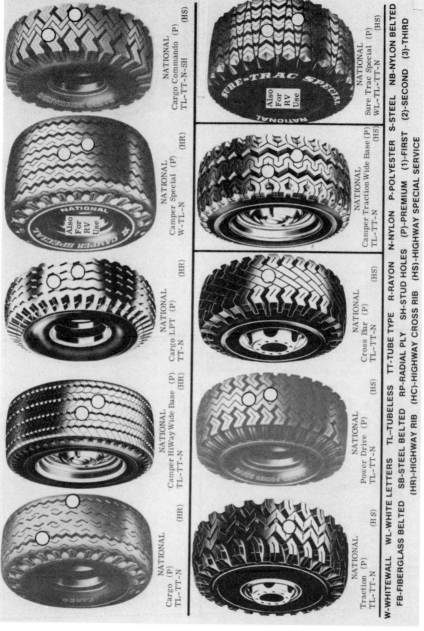

NATIONAL
Cargo (P)
TL–TT–N
(HS)

NATIONAL
Camper HiWay Wide Base (P)
TL–TT–N
(HR)

NATIONAL
Cargo LPT (P)
TT–N
(HR)

NATIONAL
Camper Special (P)
W–TL–N
(HR)

NATIONAL
Cargo Commando (P)
TL–TT–N–SH
(HS)

NATIONAL
Traction (P)
TL–TT–N
(HS)

NATIONAL
Power Drive (P)
TL–TT–N
(HS)

NATIONAL
Cross Bar (P)
TL–TT–N
(HS)

NATIONAL
Camper Traction Wide Base (P)
TL–TT–N
(HS)

NATIONAL
Sure Trac Special (P)
WL–TL–TT–N
(HS)

W–WHITEWALL  WL–WHITE LETTERS  TL–TUBELESS  TT–TUBE TYPE  R–RAYON  N–NYLON  P–POLYESTER  S–STEEL  NB–NYLON BELTED
FB–FIBERGLASS BELTED  SB–STEEL BELTED  RP–RADIAL PLY  SH–STUD HOLES  (P)–PREMIUM  (1)–FIRST  (2)–SECOND  (3)–THIRD
(HRI)–HIGHWAY RIB  (HC)–HIGHWAY CROSS RIB  (HS)–HIGHWAY SPECIAL SERVICE

**Figure 20.6.** National Camper Traction Wide Base. (*Courtesy of Al Snyder, Editor, Tire Guides Inc.*)

202

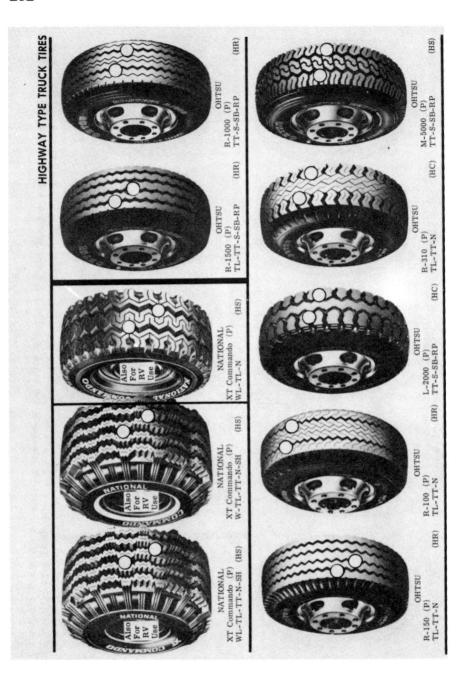

HIGHWAY TYPE TRUCK TIRES

OHTSU
R-1000 (P)
TT-S-SB-RP (HR)

OHTSU
R-1500 (P)
TL-TT-S-SB-RP (HR)

NATIONAL
XT Commando (P)
WL-TL-N (HS)

NATIONAL
XT Commando (P)
W-TL-TT-N-SH (HS)

NATIONAL
XT Commando (P)
WL-TL-TT-N-SH (HS)

OHTSU
M-5000 (P)
TT-S-SB-RP (HS)

OHTSU
R-310 (P)
TL-TT-N (HC)

OHTSU
L-2000 (P)
TT-S-SB-RP (HC)

OHTSU
R-100 (P)
TL-TT-N (HR)

OHTSU
R-150 (P)
TL-TT-N (HR)

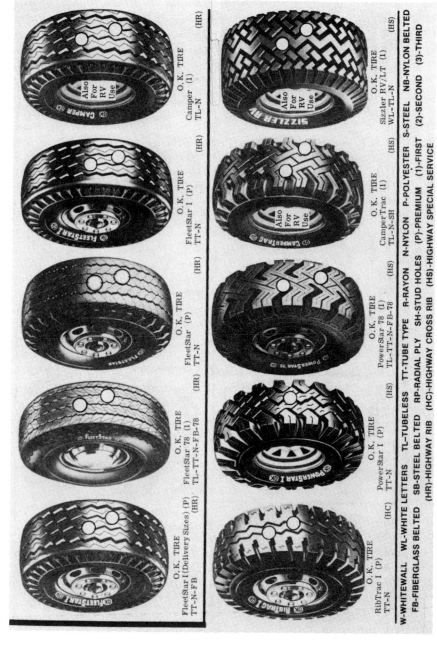

O.K. TIRE
FleetStar I(Delivery Sizes) (P)
TT-N-FB          (HR)

O.K. TIRE
FleetStar 78 (1)
TL-TT-N-FB-78   (HR)

O.K. TIRE
FleetStar (P)
TT-N            (HR)

O.K. TIRE
FleetStar I (P)
TT-N            (HR)

O.K. TIRE
Camper (1)
TL-N            (HR)

O.K. TIRE
RibTrac I (P)
TT-N            (HC)

O.K. TIRE
PowerStar I (P)
TT-N            (HS)

O.K. TIRE
PowerStar 78 (1)
TL-TT-N-FB-78   (HS)

O.K. TIRE
CamperTrac (1)
TL-N-SH         (HS)

O.K. TIRE
Sizzler RV/LT (1)
WL-TL-N         (HS)

W-WHITEWALL   WL-WHITE LETTERS   TL-TUBELESS   TT-TUBE TYPE   R-RAYON   N-NYLON   P-POLYESTER   S-STEEL   NB-NYLON BELTED
FB-FIBERGLASS BELTED   SB-STEEL BELTED   RP-RADIAL PLY   SH-STUD HOLES   (1)-PREMIUM   (1)-FIRST   (2)-SECOND   (3)-THIRD
(HR)-HIGHWAY RIB   (HC)-HIGHWAY CROSS RIB   (HS)-HIGHWAY SPECIAL SERVICE

**Figure 20.7.**   National XT Commando. *(Courtesy of Al Snyder, editor, Tire Guides Inc.)*

204

HIGHWAY TYPE TRUCK TIRES

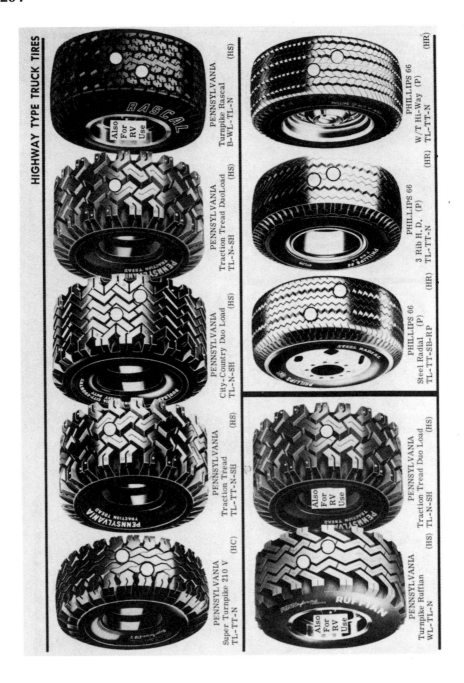

PENNSYLVANIA
Turnpike Rascal (HS)
B–WL–TL–N

PENNSYLVANIA
Traction Tread DuoLoad (HS)
TL–N–SH

PENNSYLVANIA
City-Country Duo Load (HS)
TL–N–SH

PENNSYLVANIA
Traction Tread (HS)
TL–TT–N–SH

PENNSYLVANIA
Super Turnpike 210 V (HC)
TL–TT–N

PHILLIPS 66
W/T Hi-Way (P) (HR)
TL–TT–N

PHILLIPS 66
3 Rib H.D. (P) (HR)
TL–TT–N

PHILLIPS 66
Steel Radial (P) (HR)
TL–TT–SB–RP

PENNSYLVANIA
Traction Tread Duo Load (HS)
TL–N–SH

PENNSYLVANIA
Turnpike Ruffian (HS)
WL–TL–N

205

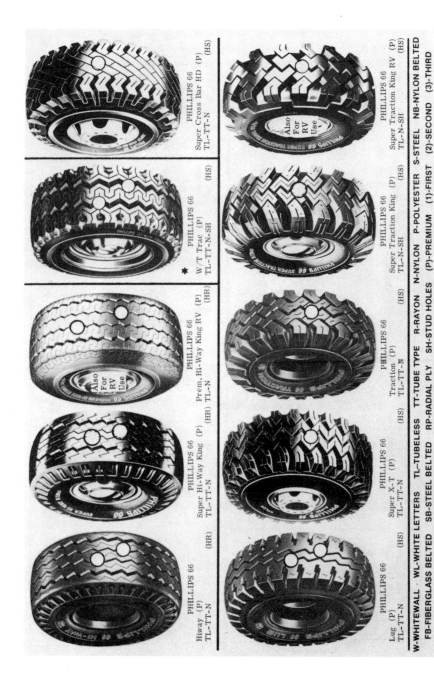

**Figure 20.8.** Phillips 66 W/T Trac. *(Courtesy of Al Snyder, editor, Tire Guides Inc.)*

# HIGHWAY TYPE TRUCK TIRES

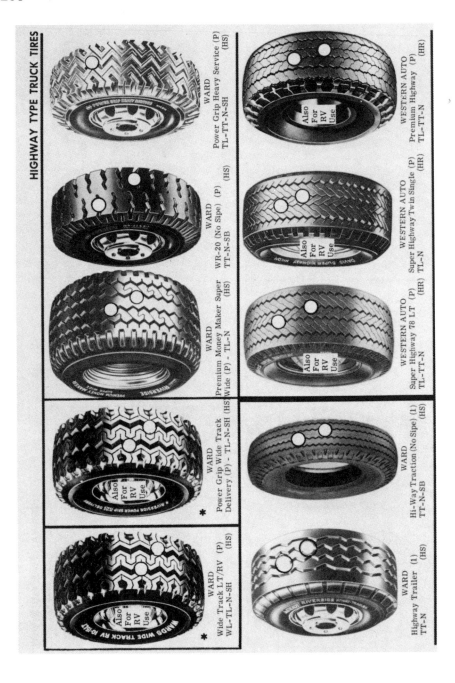

**WARD**
Power Grip Heavy Service (P)
TL-TT-N-SH (HS)

**WESTERN AUTO**
Premium Highway (P)
TL-TT-N (HR)

**WARD**
WR-20 (No Sipe) (P)
TT-N-SB (HS)

**WARD**
Premium Money Maker Super
Wide (P) - TL-N (HS)

**WESTERN AUTO**
Super Highway Twin Single (P)
TL-N (HR)

**WESTERN AUTO**
Super Highway 78 LT (P)
TL-TT-N (HR)

**WARD**
Power Grip Wide Track
Delivery (P) - TL-N-SH (HS)

**WARD**
Hi-Way Traction (No Sipe) (1)
TT-N-SB (HS)

**WARD**
Wide Track LT/RV (P)
WL-TL-N-SH (HS)

**WARD**
Highway Trailer (1)
TT-N (HS)

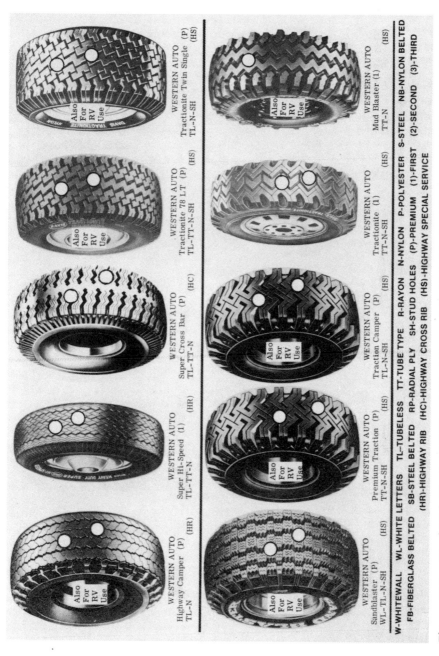

WESTERN AUTO
Highway Camper (P)    (HR)
TL–N

WESTERN AUTO
Super Hi-Speed (1)    (HR)
TL–TT–N

WESTERN AUTO
Super Cross Bar (P)    (HC)
TL–TT–N

WESTERN AUTO
Tractionite 78 LT (P)    (HS)
TL–TT–N–SH

WESTERN AUTO
Tractionite Twin Single  (P)
(HS)
TL–N–SH

WESTERN AUTO
Sandblaster (P)    (HS)
WL–TL–N–SH

WESTERN AUTO
Premium Traction (P)    (HS)
TT–N–SH

WESTERN AUTO
Traction Camper (P)    (HS)
TL–N–SH

WESTERN AUTO
Tractionite (1)    (HS)
TT–N–SH

WESTERN AUTO
Mud Blaster (1)    (HS)
TT–N

W–WHITEWALL   WL–WHITE LETTERS   TL–TUBELESS   TT–TUBE TYPE   R–RAYON   N–NYLON   P–POLYESTER   S–STEEL   NB–NYLON BELTED
FB–FIBERGLASS BELTED   SB–STEEL BELTED   RP–RADIAL PLY   SH–STUD HOLES   (P)–PREMIUM   (1)–FIRST   (2)–SECOND   (3)–THIRD
(HR)–HIGHWAY RIB   (HC)–HIGHWAY CROSS RIB   (HS)–HIGHWAY SPECIAL SERVICE

**Figure 20.9.** Ward Wide Track LT/RV and Ward Power Grip Wide Track. (*Courtesy of Al Snyder, editor, Tire Guides Inc.*)

| BRAND NAME | MANUFACTURER OR DISTRIBUTOR |
|---|---|
| MOBIL . . . . . . . . . . . . . . . . . . . . . . | KELLY-SPRINGFIELD-MOHAWK—Mobil Oil Co., 150 E. 42nd St., New York, N.Y. 10017 |
| MOBILINER . . . . . . . . . . . . . . . . . | MANSFIELD—Mobiliner, Mansfield, Ohio 44901 |
| MOHAWK . . . . . . . . . . . . . . . . . . . | MOHAWK—Mohawk Tire & Rubber Co., Hudson, Ohio 44236 |
| MONARCH . . . . . . . . . . . . . . . . . | LEE—Lee Tire & Rubber Co., Conshohocken, Pa. 19428 |
| MORRIS . . . . . . . . . . . . . . . . . . . . | ARMSTRONG—Father & Son Tire Service, Inc., 3972 Beverly Rd., Los Angeles, Calif. 90004 |
| MULTI-MILE . . . . . . . . . . . . . . . . | KELLY-SPRINGFIELD-FIRESTONE-ARMSTRONG—The Tire & Battery Corp., 4770 Hickory Hill Rd., Memphis, Tenn. 38138 |
| MUSTANG . . . . . . . . . . . . . . . . . . | ARMSTRONG—Laher Tire Co., 2615 Magnolia St., Oakland, Calif. 94607 |
| **N** NATIONAL . . . . . . . . . . . . . . . . . . | ARMSTRONG-FIRESTONE—National Tire Corp., 1035 Coffman, Longmont, Colo. 80501 |
| NORTHSTATE . . . . . . . . . . . . . . | ARMSTRONG—Sultan of Tires, 77 Coxe St., Asheville, N.C. 28801 |
| NOVA . . . . . . . . . . . . . . . . . . . . . . | GOODRICH—Javelin Tire Co., 11526 Sorrento Valley Rd., San Diego, Calif. 92122 |
| **O** O.K. TIRES . . . . . . . . . . . . . . . . . | KELLY-SPRINGFIELD-GENERAL—O.K. Tire & Rubber Co., P.O. Box 710, Ashland, Ky. 41101 |
| ORBAN . . . . . . . . . . . . . . . . . . . . | ORBAN—Kurt Orban Co., Orban Way, Wayne, N.J. 07470 |
| **P** PEERLESS . . . . . . . . . . . . . . . . . | UNIROYAL—Uniroyal, Inc., 6600 East Jefferson Ave., Detroit, Mich. 48232 |
| JC PENNEY . . . . . . . . . . . . . . . . . | DAYTON-KELLY-SPRINGFIELD-MANSFIELD-MOHAWK— J.C. Penney Co.,1301 Avenue of Americas, New York, N.Y. 10019 |
| PENNSYLVANIA . . . . . . . . . . . | MANSFIELD—Pennsylvania Tire Co., Mansfield, Ohio 44901 |
| ＊ PHILLIPS 66 . . . . . . . . . . . . . . . . | FIRESTONE-GENERAL-GOODRICH—Phillips Petroleum Co., Bartlesville, Ok. 74004 |
| PHOENIX . . . . . . . . . . . . . . . . . . | PHOENIX—Meon, Inc., 221-18 Merrick Blvd., Jamaica, N.Y. 11413 |
| PIRELLI (ITALIAN) . . . . . . . . . . | PIRELLI—Pirelli Tire Corp., 600 Third Ave., New York, N.Y. 10016 |
| PORTAGE . . . . . . . . . . . . . . . . . | SEIBERLING—Reliable Tire Co., 1115 Chestnut St., Camden N.J. 08103 |
| POS-A-TRACTION. . . . . . . . . . . | ARMSTRONG—Pos-A-Traction Industries, Inc., 622 North La Brea Ave., Inglewood, Calif. 90302 |
| PRO-TRAC . . . . . . . . . . . . . . . . . | KELLY-SPRINGFIELD—Hi-Performance Tire Co., 425 N. Robertson Blvd., Los Angeles, Calif. 90048 |
| PROWLER . . . . . . . . . . . . . . . . . | ARMSTRONG—Prowler Tire Co., 87 Whitfield Street, Guilford, Conn. 06437 |
| **R** RACEMASTER (Racing Tires) . . | DENMAN—Denman Rubber Co., Warren, Ohio 44482 |
| RAM . . . . . . . . . . . . . . . . . . . . . . | ARMSTRONG-MIMCO—77 Coxe Avenue, Asheville, N.C. 28801 |
| REGUL . . . . . . . . . . . . . . . . . . . . | GOODRICH-DENMAN—Regul Tire & Rubber Co., P.O. Box 837, Lincolnton, N.C. 28092 |
| REMINGTON . . . . . . . . . . . . . . | DUNLOP—Dunlop Tire & Rubber Co., Buffalo, N.Y. |
| REPUBLIC . . . . . . . . . . . . . . . . . | LEE—Lee Tire & Rubber Co., Conshohocken, Pa. 19428 |
| REYNOLDS . . . . . . . . . . . . . . . . | GENERAL—Reynolds Tire & Rubber Corp., 1421 38th St., Brooklyn, N.Y. 11218 |
| ROAD KING . . . . . . . . . . . . . . . | DAYTON—Dayton Tire & Rubber Co., Dayton, Ohio 45401 |
| RODGER WARD. . . . . . . . . . . . . | SEIBERLING—Rodger Ward Ent., 1739 Akron Peninsula Rd., Akron, Ohio 44813 |
| **S** SABRA (ISRAEL) . . . . . . . . . . . . | ALLIANCE—Solcoor Inc., 415 Madison Avenue, New York, NY 10017 |

**Figure 20.10.** *Who Makes It? And Where? 1978 Directory,* page 5, used to determine Phillips 66 brand name and possible manufacturer or distributor. (*Courtesy of Al Snyder, editor, Tire Guides Inc.*)

| BRAND NAME | MANUFACTURER OR DISTRIBUTOR |
|---|---|
| **U** | |
| UNION 76 . . . . . . . . . . . . . . . . . . | KELLY-SPRINGFIELD-FIRESTONE-MOHAWK—Union Oil Company of Calif., 1650 East Golf Road, Schaumburg, Ill. 60196 |
| UNIROYAL . . . . . . . . . . . . . . . . . . | UNIROYAL—Uniroyal, Inc., 6600 East Jefferson Avenue, Detroit, Mich. 48232 |
| UNIROYAL/EUROPE . . . . . . . . . | UNIROYAL—Uniroyal International, Oxford Management & Research Ctr., Middlebury, Conn. 06749 |
| UNITED . . . . . . . . . . . . . . . . . . . | MANSFIELD—Dealers United Inc., P.O. Drawer S, Macon, Ga. 31202 |
| **V** | |
| VANGUARD . . . . . . . . . . . . . . . . | GOODRICH-Reliable Tire Co., 1115 Chestnut St., Camden, NJ 08103 |
| VAN NESS . . . . . . . . . . . . . . . . . | ARMSTRONG—East Bay Tire Co., 225 Third Street, Oakland, Calif. 94607 |
| VEITH . . . . . . . . . . . . . . . . . . . . | VEITH—Intermark Tire Co., 600 Third Avenue, New York, N.Y. 10016 |
| VELOCE* . . . . . . . . . . . . . . . . . . | DUNLOP—Veloce Tire Corp., 15990 Shady Grove Rd., Gaithersburg, Md. 20760 |
| VELTRO (ITALY) . . . . . . . . . . . . | CEAT-CEAT—S.p.A. Pneumatici, Casella Postale 509, 10100 Torino, Italy |
| VETTA . . . . . . . . . . . . . . . . . . . . | ARMSTRONG—Vetta Tire & Rubber Co., P.O. Box 857, Macon, Ga. 31203 |
| VICTORIAN . . . . . . . . . . . . . . . . | UNIROYAL-MANSFIELD—Victorian Tire Assoc., 8705 Katy Freeway, Houston, Texas 77024 |
| VOGUE . . . . . . . . . . . . . . . . . . . | KELLY-SPRINGFIELD—Kelly-Springfield Tire Co., Cumberland, Md. 21502 |
| VREDESTEIN (HOLLAND) . . . . . | VREDESTEIN—Vredestein, P.O. Box 27, Enschede, Holland |
| **W-X-Y-Z** | |
| * WARD (MONT. WARD) . . . . . . . . | FIRESTONE, KELLY-SPRINGFIELD—Montgomery Ward & Co., Montgomery Ward Plaza, Chicago, Ill. 60671 |
| WESTERN AUTO . . . . . . . . . . . . . | DAYTON-KELLY-SPRINGFIELD-MOHAWK—Western Auto Supply Co., 2107 Grand Ave., Kansas City, Mo. 64108 |
| WHITE . . . . . . . . . . . . . . . . . . . . | DAYTON—White Stores Inc., 3910 Callfield Rd., Wichita Falls, Texas 76308 |
| WINDSOR . . . . . . . . . . . . . . . . . | MANSFIELD—Schenuit Tire & Rubber Co., 9 W. Aylesbury Rd., Timonium, Md. 21093 |
| XPRES . . . . . . . . . . . . . . . . . . . . | ARMSTRONG—Keil's, 11th & Tatnall Sts., Wilmington, Del. 19801 |
| YOKOHAMA (JAPAN) . . . . . . . . . | YOKOHAMA—Yokohama Tire Corp., 1530 Church Road, Montebello, Calif. 90640 |
| YORK (JAPAN) . . . . . . . . . . . . . | YOKOHAMA—Yokohama Tire Corp., 1530 Church Road, Montebello, Calif. 90640 |
| ZENITH . . . . . . . . . . . . . . . . . . . | SEIBERLING—Seiberling Rubber Co., Barberton, Ohio 44203 |

*Some Lines Manufactured by Other Companies

**Figure 20.11.** *Who Makes It? And Where? 1978 Directory,* page 7, used to determine Ward brand name and possible manufacturer or distributor. *(Courtesy of Al Snyder, editor, Tire Guides Inc.)*

**Figure 20.12.** Suspect's test impression in workshop test case. (*Courtesy of Luis Bautista, Deputy Sheriff, Riverside County Sheriff, Indio, Calif.*)

**Figure 20.13.** Mold drawing with arrows pointing to the stud hole locations in workshop test case. (*Courtesy of Firestone Tire & Rubber Co.*)

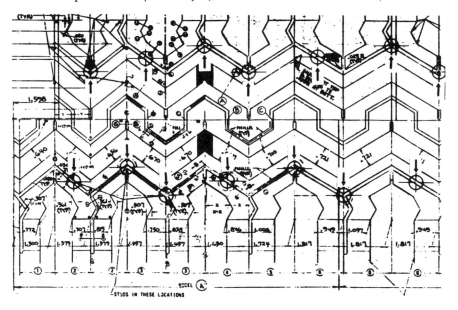

This test case example also highlights the stud-hole feature. The mold drawing (Figure 20.13) has arrows pointing to the stud-hole locations. The crime scene imprint (see Figure 20.1) also has arrows pointing to the same stud-hole locations. To accommodate studs, tires have a post protruding out of the mold, resulting in a hole in the tire. Each hole has a stabilized area around it for support. These locations are purposely not aligned, giving a multitude of traction paths for a better bite on hard-packed snow or ice. Stud holes are generally located in the shoulder area, where the loading is greatest.

## Question 4

Using the *Who Makes It? and Where? Directory*, list the single most logical manufacturer of this design to contact for tread drawings. (Referring to the appropriate directory pages [Figures 20.10 and 20.11] yields the answer.)

---

## Answer

| Brand | Manufacturer or distributor |
| --- | --- |
| Phillips 66 | Firestone, General, Goodrich |
| Ward (Montgomery Ward) | Firestone, Kelly-Springfield |

Firestone is the most logical to contact because it is listed as a supplier for both brands. Firestone designed and manufactured this tread pattern. Tires were also manufactured by General, Goodrich, and Kelly-Springfield in 1978. Mold sideplates were stamped with many different names for each account. A look at the *Tread Design Guide* makes it obvious that the examiners must be thorough.

Additional questions require an understanding of tread drawings to determine the rate of wear. These have been omitted because detail is not clear enough at a reduced scale. The examiner is then asked to locate the screen positive overlay properly, looking for specific accidental characteristics that are consistent on the test impression.

The final question is: "Would this comparison of specific accidental characteristics be satisfactory for a positive identification?" For those who did their homework and have a keen eye, the answer is *yes.*

# Glossary

*Accidental characteristics:* Tire wear features and damage.

*Aging:* Weathering of tire due to effects of atmospheric conditions.

*Alignment:* Adjustment of various parts of the steering mechanism for most efficient operation of wheels and vehicle.

*Aquaplaning: See* Hydroplaning.

*Aspect ratio:* The ratio of the section height of the tire to the section width.

*Balance:* The uniformity of mass distribution of a tire relative to its spin and steer axes.

*Bead:* The portion of the tire that fits onto the rim of the wheel.

*Belt:* A reinforcing member, usually consisting of one or more plies, located circumferentially around the tire and under the tread.

*Bias angle:* The angle of the cords in a tire with respect to the tire centerline.

*Bias belted tire:* A pneumatic tire structure of bias-ply (diagonal) type in which the carcass is restricted by a belt.

*Bias tire (diagonal):* A pneumatic tire in which the ply cords extending to the beads are laid at alternate angles substantially less than 90 degrees to the centerline of the tread.

*Bladder:* In the curing press, the tire is fit onto the bladder, an internal bag that contains steam or hot water that will force the tire into the mold.

*Camber:* The tilt of the front wheels of a vehicle. Outward at top from perpendicular is positive camber; inward at top is negative camber.

*Carcass:* The tire structure, except the tread and the sidewall rubber.

*Casing:* A used tire to which additional tread rubber may be attached for the purpose of retreading.

*Centerline:* The circumference of a tire at the middle of the tread.

*Chunking:* Loss of pieces of tread rubber resulting from high-speed operation, excessive movement of tread elements, or hardened rubber elements.

*Class characteristics:* Features common to one specific tire design or mold.

*Conicity:* The built-in tendency of a tire to roll in a direction not parallel to the vehicle direction, as if the tire were a cone rolling on its side.

*Contact patch: See* Footprint.

*Cord:* The strands forming the plies in a tire.

*Cracking:* The initiation and propagation of fissures in tire rubber.

*Cross-rib tire:* A drive-wheel position tire with grooves that extend radially into the shoulder.

*Curb scuffing:* Abrasion of the shoulder and sidewall of a tire caused by rubbing, as in parking against a curb. With white sidewall tires, scuffing may remove black veneer, exposing white rubber.

*Curing: See* Vulcanization.

*Decoupling groove:* A circumferential shoulder groove next to the tire sidewall.

*Deflection:* The difference between the unloaded and the loaded section heights.

*Dual assembly:* Two wheels mounted side by side on one end of an axle.

*Dynamic balance:* Equal distribution of weight on the left and right side of the tire centerline.

*Even wear:* Uniform abrasion across the tread surface.

*Feathering:* A condition where edges of the tire tread ribs have feather edges.

*Flatness:* The contour of the tire tread from shoulder to shoulder; the tread radius.

*Flatspotting:* A flattening in the tire footprint area during parking that results in short-term ride disturbance.

*Flotation:* The ability of a tire to sustain a vehicle under soft footprint conditions.

*Footprint:* The shape and area of that portion of the tire in contact with the ground.

*General accidental characteristics:* Normal tire wear.

*Grooves:* Channels between the tread ribs.

*Growth:* The gradual increase in tire size over a period of time due to the effect of inflation pressure and service conditions.

*Hydroplaning:* Partial or total loss of contact of the tire with the road due to floating action caused by surface water.

*Inflation pressure:* The amount of compressed air in a tire.

*Innerliner:* The airtight layer(s) forming the inside surface of a tubeless tire.

*Load range:* A system formerly used to designate the load-carrying capacity of a tire.

*Load rating:* The maximum load a tire is rated to carry at a specified inflation pressure.

*Lugs:* Discontinuous radial rows of tread rubber elements in direct contact with the road surface.

*Mean ground contact pressure:* The tire load divided by the footprint area.

*Mud and snow tires:* Passenger and light truck tires designed to provide better starting, stopping, and driving performance in snow conditions than non-MS tires.

*Noise:* The sound generated by a tire and transmitted to the occupants of a vehicle—e.g., joint slap, pitch tone, squeal, whine, rumble. Noise may be airborne or transmitted through the vehicle.

*Noise treatment:* The arrangement of different pitch lengths of the tread elements around the circumference of a tire, to reduce noise.

*Nonskid:* Depth of the grooves in a tire tread.

*Pitch length:* The circumferential distance from one repeating point in a tread pattern to the next.

*Pitch sequence: See* Noise treatment.

*Ply:* A layer of rubber-coated parallel cords.

*Pneumatic tire:* A mechanical device made of rubber, chemicals, fabric, steel or other materials, which when mounted on an automotive wheel provides the traction and contains the gas or fluid that sustains the load.

*Point height:* The vertical distance from the valley to the highest point on one side of a tread rib.

*Pressure rise:* The increase in inflation pressure due to heat buildup during dynamic operation of a tire.

*Profile:* Cross-section.

*PSI:* Pounds of internal force per square inch.

*Radial tire:* A pneumatic tire in which the ply cords that extend to the bead are laid substantially at a 90-degree angle to the centerline of the tread, the carcass being stabilized by an essentially inextensible circumferential belt.

*Retreading:* The process of renewing the tread on a tire by buffing the old surface and applying new rubber.

*Ribs:* Generally circumferential rows of tread rubber.

*Rim:* A support, usually metal, for a tire or a tire and tube assembly on which the tire beads are seated.

*Rim flange:* The part of the tire rim that supports the bead in a lateral direction.

*Rolling radius:* The distance of the axle from the road surface on a moving tire.

*Rolling resistance:* The retarding force created within a tire opposite to the direction of rotation.

*Section height:* The distance between tread crown and bead seat when a tire is inflated but not under load.

*Section width:* The distance across a tire at widest part when inflated but not under load.

*Sidewall:* The portion of a tire between the tread and the bead.

*Sinkage:* Compression of soil due to pressure from the tire footprint.

*Sipes:* The narrow slots that subdivide tread elements to improve traction characteristics.

*Skid resistance:* The ability of a tire to maintain a grip on the road and resist slide and slip.

*Slip:* Differential in magnitude or direction between the circumferential velocity of a tire at the contact surface and velocity of travel.

*Slip angle:* The deviation between the plane of rotation and the direction of travel of a tire.

*Specific accidental characteristics:* Unique damage features in an exact location of a tire.

*Squeal:* The high-pitched noise associated with the slippage between the tire and the road surface during stopping, starting, or cornering.

*Squiggle:* The phenomenon that occurs when the circumferential tire rib widths correspond to longitudinal highway groove spacing.

*Squirm:* The movement of the tread as the tire rotates.

*Static loaded radius:* The distance of the axle from the road surface on a stationary, or nonrolling, tire.

*Stone retention:* The characteristic of a tread design to capture and hold loose stones.

*Tandem:* Tires set one immediately behind the other.

*Tie-bars:* Stabilizing rubber interruptions of grooves below the tread surface.

*Toe-in:* Adjustment of front wheels so that they are slightly closer together at the front than at the back.

*Torque:* The basic tire function of transmitting force from the drive axle to the ground contact area.

*Track:* A tire tread path.

*Tracking:* The ability of a tire to continue moving in a straight path.

*Traction:* The ability of a tire to grip the road and generate propulsive forces for driving, lateral forces for cornering, and retarding forces for braking.

*Tread:* The portion of a tire that comes in contact with the road.

*Tread depth: See* Nonskid.

*Tread element:* Rubber portion of tread, bound by grooves, slots, and/or noncontained sipes.

*Tread life:* Length of service until the tire wears out.

*Tread pressure:* The distribution of load across the footprint area of a tire.

*Tread radius: See* Flatness.

*Treadwear:* The progressive wearing-away of a tire in service due to abrasion on the road surface.

*Tread wear indicators:* Narrow bars of rubber molded at a height of one-sixteenth of an inch across the bottom of the tread grooves. When the tread wears down to these bars, the tire should be replaced.

*Vulcanization:* The process of cross-linking a rubber compound through heat and pressure.

*Weathering: See* Aging.

*Wear bars: See* Tread wear indicators.

*Whine:* The airborne noise associated with movement of the tread elements of a tire on the road surface.

# References

Bantle, Manfred, and Helmuth Bott. 1988. *The Porsche 959 Automotive Technology International.* London: Redwood Web Offset.

Bodziak, William J. Slide presentation at International Association of Forensic Sciences, Vancouver, B.C., Canada, August 27, 1987.

Cassidy, Michael J. 1980. *Footwear Identification.* Ottawa, Ont., Canada: Royal Canadian Mounted Police.

Firestone. 1982. *Passenger Tire Sales Handbook.* Akron, Ohio: Firestone Sales Training Department.

Fletcher, John E. January 1985. "A Picture Is Worth a Thousand Words." *Technical Photography.*

Geberth, Vernon J. 1983. *Practical Homicide Investigation.* New York: Elsevier Science Publishing Co.

Genck, Wayne J. 1987. "Trial Success Linked to Meeting Expert Witnesses' Expectations." *The Expert and the Law: A Publication of the National Forensic Center 7/2.* Lawrenceville, N.J.

Given, B. W., R. B. Nehrich, and J. C. Shields. 1977. *Tire Tracks and Tread Marks.* Houston: Gulf Publishing Co.

Grieve, David L. The identification process; Attitude and approach. *Journal of Forensic Identification 38/5* (Sept./Oct. 1988). The official publication of the International Association for Identification.

Grogan, R. J. 1971. Tyres and crime. *Journal of the Forensic Science Society 11/1* (Jan. 1971). Fort Dunlop, Birmingham, England.

Grogan, R. J. 1978. Tyre Marks as Evidence. Paper presented to the Eighth International Association of Forensic Sciences, Wichita, Kansas, May 1978. Birmingham, England: Tire Technical Division Dunlop Limited.

Howell, Bonnie. 1988. Correspondence from the Institute of Police Technology and Management, Jacksonville, Fla.

Huber, Roy A. 1959–60. "Expert Witnesses." *Criminal Law Quarterly 2/280.* Toronto: Cartwright & Sons, Ltd.

Hyzer, W. G. 1986. Tech talk. *Photomethods 29/9* (Sept. 1986).

Hyzer, W. G. 1981. Scientific instrumentation. *Photomethods* 24/7 (July 1981).

Kovac, F. J. 1978. *Tire Technology.* 5th ed. Akron, Ohio: Goodyear Tire & Rubber Co.

Law and Order. 1981. Tire "footprints" help solve homicide cases. Chicago, Ill.

McDonald, Peter. 1984. *Display.* Los Angeles: Museum of Science and Industry.

Michigan State Police. 1982. *The Identification of Vehicles from Wheelbase and Tire Tread Measurements.* East Lansing, Mich.: East Lansing Forensic Laboratory.

Nause, L. A. 1987. *The Science of Tire Impression Identification.* Ottawa, Ont.: RCMP Gazette.

Parker, Tom. 1985. *In One Day.* Boston: Houghton Mifflin.

Poynter, Dan. 1987. *The Expert Witness Handbook.* Santa Barbara Calif.: Para.

Resources Development Corporation. 1970. *Tire Performance and Construction.* East Lansing, Mich.: RDC.

*Rubber & Plastic News.* 1987. *The Global Tire Market.* Akron, Ohio.

Rubber Manufacturers Association. 1987. *Care and Service of Automobile Tires.* Washington, D.C.: RMA.

Time Inc. 1967. *Wheels.* Life Science Library. New York: Time Inc.

Tire Guides, 1978 & 1981. *Tread Design Guide, Who Makes It? and Where?* Boca Raton, Fla.: Bennett Garfield.

Truszkowski, Gary J. 1988. *Journal of Forensic Identification.* Official publication of the International Association for Identification.

# Index

*Peter McDonald* is a tire print identification specialist, formerly manager of Tire Design at the Firestone Tire & Rubber Company, in Akron, Ohio. With twenty-eight years of experience in tire design and now as a leader in tire forensics, Mr. McDonald has taught at the FBI Academy, The Canadian Investigation Society, The International Association of Forensic Scientists, International Association for Identification, American Society for Industrial Security, and police academies for forensic scientists.

He has written for *Police Times* and *Law and Order*. Articles have been published about him in *Time, People Magazine,* and *Rubber World,* to mention a few. He is a member of the American Academy of Forensic Sciences, International Association for Identification, and the Akron Rubber Group. He has a degree in architecture from Miami University in Ohio and has been awarded six tire patents. He is certified by the Ohio Peace Officers Training Council and actively trains examiners and reviews and testifies in cases.